FINANCIAL PLANNING

from **WE** *to* **ME:**

Divorce Strategies to Help You Get
More of What You Want

Kathleen L. Cotton
Certified Financial Planner

with Ellen J. Webber, CFP

𝕴𝖊𝖆𝖑𝖙𝖍 𝕭𝖔𝖔𝖐𝖘

While a great deal of care has been taken to provide accurate information, the ideas, suggestions, general principals and conclusions presented in this book are subject to local, state, and federal laws and regulations, court cases and any revisions of same. This publication is sold with the understanding that the publisher and the authors are not engaged in rendering legal, accounting, or other professional services. The reader is thus urged to consult legal or financial counsel regarding any points of law.

FINANCIAL PLANNING *from* WE *to* ME: Divorce Strategies to Help You Get More of What You Want: Copyright 1996 by Kathleen L. Cotton, CFP with Ellen J. Webber, CFP

Published by Wealth Books, 4208 198th St. S.W., #202, Lynnwood, WA 98036. Printed in the United States of America. All rights reserved. No part of this publication may be reproduced, stored in a retrieval system, or transmitted in any form or by any means, electronic, mechanical, photocopy, recording, or otherwise without prior written permission of the publisher and the copyright holder.

Publisher's Cataloging in Publication
    (Prepared by Quality Books Inc.)

Cotton, Kathleen L.
    Financial planning from we to me: divorce strategies to help you get more of what you want / Kathleen L. Cotton : with Ellen J. Webber. —Lynnwood, WA : Wealth Books, 1996
    p. cm.
    Includes bibliographical references.
    ISBN 0-9618700-2-8

    1. Finance, Personal. 2. Equitable distribution of marital property. 3. Divorce settlements. I. Title.
HG179.C68 1996   332.024
                                                        QBI95-20373

Also by Kathleen L. Cotton
Financial Planning For The Not Yet Wealthy
Spend Your Way To Wealth

By
Kathleen L. Cotton and Rachel W. Paysse
Keys To Controlling Your Financial Destiny

𝔚𝔢𝔞𝔩𝔱𝔥 𝔅𝔬𝔬𝔨𝔰

are available at a discount with bulk purchases for education, business, premium or sales promotion use. For single book purchases, see order form in back of book. For information on bulk order discounts, write or call:

𝔚𝔢𝔞𝔩𝔱𝔥 𝔅𝔬𝔬𝔨𝔰
4208 198th Street S.W., #202
Lynnwood, WA 98036 1-206-672-6050

ACCOLADES

We could not have published this book without the help of willing readers and critics who helped us "polish" up the text—technically and for ease of understanding. These readers went out of their way to point out differences of opinions in gray areas of the law and reminded us of areas we forgot to cover or where we said too much. Additionally, they helped us clean up our sometimes too colloquial English, and at least two of our readers provided grammatical editing.

They are Carol Ann Wilson, Quantum Financial, Boulder Colorado; Cicily Maton, Aequus, Chicago, Illinois; Patrick Farley, Protocol, Saint Paul, Minnesota; Eric Olson, Jonson, Hurley, Olson & Olson; Seattle, WA; Jennifer Stevens, Tim Edwards & Associates, Auburn WA; Ruth Robinson, Attorney at Law, Everett, WA; Linda Roubik, Wechsler, Besk, Erickson; Ross & Roubik, Seattle, WA, and Shirley F. Wendle, M.A., Edmonds, WA.

Credit goes also to Shirley F. Wendle, M.A. for providing the foundation of information for Chapter 20, How to Choose a Therapist. Shirley is a practicing therapist located in Edmonds, Washington.

Additionally we had a creative illustrator, Debbie Olson of Lake Forest Park, WA, and talented cover artist, David Marty of Edmonds, WA. The finished product was typeset by Danielle Clarneaux of Bellevue, WA.

BEFORE WE BEGIN…

If you are reading this book, you probably have divorce on your mind and it's no wonder—divorce strikes more often than the common cold. In fact, it strikes about five out of every ten homes in every neighborhood, except maybe Hollywood where everything is bigger than life, including divorce. No doubt about it—we are surrounded by divorcing individuals.

Divorce is not easy and isn't entered into nearly as easily as marriage. Sometimes it takes both parties years to make the final decision and occasionally only one party is privy to these thoughts which are one day pulled out of a hat. However it occurs, it is not pleasant. It is expensive, frustrating, emotionally devastating, and time consuming. That is, if one party wants something that the other has already put dubs on.

A fair and equitable divorce is the goal—unfortunately, that goal is often difficult to obtain. The outcome, however, can be influenced by careful and methodical planning. The first step is to evaluate in detail one's financial needs, consider any financial penalties, such as lower income due to forfeited careers as a result of the marriage, have major assets such as real estate, pensions, and businesses valued by professionals, be smart about dividing retirement pension accounts, and be realistic—ask for property which will meet your needs. And, if there are children, don't forget that property and spousal/child support settlements agreed to in the heat of anger or at a stalemated negotiating session will also impact them for years to come.

Most of the information in this book is pertinent to both men and women, although in a few cases you will find circumstances that are applicable more often to one gender than the other. Our hope by writing this book is that we can help make the divorce experience a little easier on you or someone you know. At the time same, we hope you will gain knowledge—a lot or a little—to be used now or stored for future use.

FINANCIAL PLANNING *from* WE *to* ME

Preface

1 CHAPTER ONE—DIVORCE MYTHS AND MYSTERIES
Surviving The Stages, You Are The Key, The Last Curtain Call, Ten Most Common Myths, Myth 1: No fault is no hassle; Myth 2: I get half of everything; Myth 3: If my income is less, I'll automatically receive alimony; Myth 4: I have the kids so I should keep the house; Myth 5: I'm the mother, so I get custody of the children; Myth 6: I don't have to worry about health insurance because I'm still covered by my former spouse's plan; Myth 7: If my spouse is assigned the debt, I am off the hook; Myth 8: My spouse and I can remain friends; Myth 9: I'll get more if I get him/her in front of the judge; Myth 10: Any attorney can do a good job on my divorce.

15 CHAPTER TWO—FROM WE TO ME NEEDS
Taming The Cash Flow Crisis, Hot On The Trail, Separate Your Expenses, Curb The Credit Card Risk, Bulletproof Your Foundation, Three Expenses Scenarios, Worksheet 2A: Living Expenses

21 CHAPTER THREE—TUG OF WAR
Parenting Plan, Child Support By The Schedule, Tinkering with The Formulas, The College Dilemma, Juggling Tax Exemptions, Child Support Worksheets, Example 3A—Sam & Sally Smith, Worksheet 3A: Child Support Calculation

33 CHAPTER FOUR—INCOME SHARING
The Case For Support, Retraining Options, IRS Supplied Pain Pill, IRA Contributions, Cohabitation Or Remarriage Issues, Alimony Trusts, Loose Ends, Example 4A: A Spoonful Of Sugar Helps The Medicine Go Down, Example 4B

41 CHAPTER FIVE—SLICING THE MARITAL PIE
Mine-Yours-Ours, Typical Marital Assets, Business Difficulties, Invisible Assets, Mystery Assets, Don't Forget The Pension, House Trap Doors, A Word On Taxes, An Exception To Tax Free Transfers, Drafting Your Game Plan, Worksheet 5A: Joint Property Assets

51 CHAPTER SIX—MY MOM GAVE IT TO ME
Marital Unless Proven Otherwise, Tainting Separate Assets, Worksheet 6A: Separate Assets

55 CHAPTER SEVEN—MARITAL DEBTS AND OTHER LIABILITIES
Common Debts, Helpful Hints On Marital Debts, Credit Card Traps, General Cautions, Worksheet 7A: Joint Liabilities

61 CHAPTER EIGHT—THE ROOF OVER YOUR HEAD
Avoiding A Nasty Tax Surprise, Purchasing A Replacement Residence, The $125,000 Solution, Example 8A: Sam & Sally Smith Residence Sale, Worksheet 8A: Residence Sales Tax Calculations

69 CHAPTER NINE—DIVIDING THE RETIREMENT NEST EGG WITHOUT BREAKING THE YOLK
It's Your Money Too, Nailing Down The Values, Change Of IRA Ownership, SEPP Your IRA, Dividing A Future Pension Annuity, Present Value Of Future Pension, Years Of Marriage/Years Of Service Formula, Future Pension Issues, Example 9A: Military Pension Plan Present Value Calculation

79 CHAPTER TEN—PATHWAYS TO THE FUTURE
Career Resuscitation, The High Cost Of Not Working, My Story, The $64,000 Question, Career Counselors Can Put Life In Your Workday, Example 10A: Quantification Of Career Opportunity Cost To Marital Community And Discounted Wage Potential Due To Child Care/Homemaker Commitment, Example 10B: Future Earnings Projection Compared With Potential Opportunity Cost Due To Lack Of Work Experience

87 CHAPTER ELEVEN—WHOSE BALLOON'S BIGGER?
Crumbs From Social Security, Collecting On Your EX, It's Not Fair

91 CHAPTER TWELVE—OVER MY DEAD BODY
Will You or Won't You, Own A Piece of Their Rock, Life Insurance Premiums As Alimony, Negotiate For Life

95 CHAPTER THIRTEEN—A COBRA YOU CAN LOVE
Comparing Policies, Self Insured Plans, Insuring The Children

99 CHAPTER FOURTEEN—YOUR FAIR SHARE CAMPAIGN
Use It Or Lose It, Vacations, Sick Pay And Other Niceities Of Life, Financial Savvy, Career Costs, Work May Not Be In The Cards, Long Term Marriage, The 50/50 Result, The 60/40 Result, The 60/40 Plus Spousal Support Result, Reality Check, Worksheet 14A: Personal Documents Required For Long Term Analysis

111 **CHAPTER FIFTEEN—HOW AM I GOING TO GET THROUGH THIS MESS?**
Can You Settle, Determine Your Negotiating Potential, Build A Team

115 **CHAPTER SIXTEEN—CAN YOU AVOID GOING TO TRIAL**
Should You Keep The Reins

117 **CHAPTER SEVENTEEN—ODDS AND IMPORTANT ENDS**
How will I file my income tax returns during the divorce period? Do I have to keep my married name? Do I need to have an attorney to get a divorce? Can my spouse and I share an attorney? Who determines how much child support will be paid? How do I collect child support from the non-custodial parent if they quit paying? What if my spouse leaves and takes all the money? What can I do to reduce legal costs? Are my legal fees tax deductible? What if my spouse doesn't give me the total due for both child support and alimony? Will I have to pay taxes on any assets or property transferred to me as a result of the property division? Do I have to pay taxes on my spousal maintenance? Are gifts considered joint property? Should I go through a mediation process? Should I see a therapist? Why can't my attorney give me financial advice?

125 **CHAPTER EIGHTEEN—CHOOSING YOUR ATTORNEY**
Ask Other Professionals, The Third Degree, Remember It's Your Future

129 **CHAPTER NINETEEN—CHOOSING A FINANCIAL ADVISOR**
Needle In The Haystack, Sleuthing For Value, Take Care

133 **CHAPTER TWENTY—CHOOSING A THERAPIST**
Getting Help, Theraputic Probes

137 **CHAPTER TWENTY ONE—AFTER THE DARK, COMES LIGHT**
Help Yourself, Create A Spending Plan, Important Issues For Today, You May Need A Financial Professional, Moving Forward

153 **RESOURCE DIRECTORY**

155 **GLOSSARY**

ix

CHAPTER ONE
Divorce Myths And Mysteries

"Trailer for sale or rent, rooms to let, fifty cents," sang Roger Miller during the '60s. Perhaps he, too, was going through a divorce. Today, the same tune is being sung by many people—houses for sale and rooms to rent. While divorces back then weren't quite as numerous as today, marriage has always been one of the great casualties of modern life. Just look around your neighborhood. Chances are you can count at least one or two homes up for sale due to marital breakups. And some who keep their homes will be taking in roommates.

More people than ever before are getting divorced. Statistically speaking, a person marrying today has a 50/50 chance of facing the "BIG D." Each year in the United States over 1.1 million divorces are initiated. My practice is located in the state of Washington, and here the story is the same as evidenced by the following information. The last column is the ratio of marriages to divorces.

YEAR	(1) MARRIAGES	(2) DIVORCES	RATIO (1) to (2)
1985	43,771	25,512	1.6
1986	43,255	25,990	1.6
1987	43,503	27,216	1.6
1988	44,922	25,836	1.7
1989	45,278	26,683	1.6
1990	46,492	28,240	1.6
1991	46,103	29,683	1.5
1992	45,481	29,803	1.5
1993	44,380	29,515	1.5
1994	43,624	29,771	1.4

Source: Washington State Department of Health

The risk is even greater for second and subsequent marriages.

This book has been written to help those people who are facing the inevitable and want to be prepared. A divorce can unquestionably be emotionally devastating, traumatic and painful. Your future, though, can be better than you think if you go into this divorce with clear ideas about what you need and how you are going to get it.

Surviving The Stages

To start, the best way for you to deal with a divorce is to understand the stages you will go through and the actions necessary for financial survival. One of the first things that should become evident is that most individuals really endure three divorces—the emotional, the physical, and the financial/legal. Each and every stage has its impact on the pocketbook.

The emotional divorce comes first and may have started years ago for one or both spouses. During the onset of this stage, marriage counselors may have been on your appointment calendar. Next comes the physical separation. Two households are now trying to live on the same dollars once used to support just one. If you are the spouse who has elected to leave the family homestead, you are also on unfamiliar turf. If you stayed in the family home, you may be trying to meet high mortgage and utility payments on a much lower income. The third and final divorce you must survive is the most important to your future financial security—the legal division of the financial assets and income streams. This third stage is the most critical. Expert advice is mandatory. Without competent legal counsel and good financial advice, you could unknowingly forfeit thousands of dollars and jeopardize your lifestyle not only today but also in the years to come.

You Are The Key

You hold the key to your future, not your attorney or the judge that may possibly hear the case. They can't predict your future. At best, your attorney can only make an educated guess at how any particular settlement might impact you. When the divorce is over they are no longer involved in your future. You, and you alone, must be responsible for doing all you can to ensure that the settlement you receive won't financially bankrupt you in the years to come. This applies to both men and women—women often receive too little to make up for income disparities between themselves and their spouses, and men may give away too much in a misguided attempt to buy their children's love and respect.

Other players in a dissolution case may include mental health and occupational counselors, accountants, appraisers, financial planners, and your spouse and his or her attorney. Financial experts are almost always mandatory if you want to evaluate the long term effects of the asset and income tradeoffs involved in dividing the balance sheets. The separation of two individuals is significantly more complex than the phrase "splitting the sheets" implies. You are in fact breaking up a business partnership and, as such, it takes careful analysis, coolheaded decisions, and competent professional assistance.

The Last Curtain Call

Divorce is an expensive solution to family difficulties. But it may be the last curtain call in a play with too many acts. In the end, it comes down to economics—what is the value of the community, who gets what, and how are the buyout terms structured. One of the harsh realities many people have to face is that the earning power of one spouse may be one of the major assets of the marriage. When this is the case, financial concerns such as arriving at an equitable property settlement, dealing with new levels of income and expenses, and avoiding costly financial mistakes become of the utmost concern. What appears to be an equitable settlement today may turn out to be far from equitable five or ten years down the road.

In many cases, people let erroneous beliefs lead them into poor decisions and unpleasant surprises. Attempts to find your way through the maze of legal and financial considerations involved in a dissolution may fail simply because you do not know what questions to ask. The goal of this book is to help provide answers to some of the more common areas of concern that you need to be aware of during the divorce process.

Chapter One—Divorce Myths And Mysteries

Ten Most Common Myths

First, we will deal with 10 of the most common myths surrounding divorce, and then we will provide you with the tools to be an informed, organized, and efficient partner with your attorney. This part of the process will be effective in limiting the amount of money you spend for your attorney to perform tasks you could be doing yourself.

MYTH 1
No fault is no hassle

While you may be able to fill a book with "faults" of which your spouse is guilty, most states, Washington among them, do not care. Guilt and punishment are no longer the name of the game. No matter that your spouse has run up endless debts, dallied with your best friend, come home drunk too many times and verbally or physically abused you. Activities like these do their damage to a marriage, but they don't aid you when you are trying to justify a bigger share of the marital assets.

As an example, Washington State's no-fault law views marriage as an economic partnership and does not care who did what. Both the husband and wife are assumed to share equally in the benefits of the partnership regardless of who earns the income. This makes negotiating over assets the name of the game. All of the property is before the court, so to speak, for "just and equitable division" irrespective of whether it is community or separate property. This means that nearly any type of property division can be made if both parties agree to it. While you may not feel you'll ever be able to agree, over 90% of divorcing couples eventually do settle and avoid a potentially bitter and expensive court battle.

MYTH 2
I get half of everything

Each spouse has a right to share in the joint property acquired during the marriage. Generally gifts or inheritances are considered separate property of the person who received them, but this assumption can be erroneous if the separate asset is commingled with joint assets. Getting fair compensation for separate dollars that were used to buy marital assets generally requires good records and diligent detective work to trace the funds. If large sums of money are involved, it may be very worthwhile to undertake an effort in this area.

If the marriage is long term (20 years or more) and one spouse is economically disadvantaged due to health, lack of job skills, earning power, etc., that spouse may end up receiving a greater share of the marital property to compensate for their lack of earning power. A short term marriage, in contrast, is more likely to end up in a 50/50 split of the marital assets.

Chapter One—Divorce Myths And Mysteries

MYTH 3
If my income is less, I'll automatically receive alimony

This is far from an automatic right. It is probable that spousal support (also called maintenance) might be awarded if you have been out of the workforce for years, intend to pursue necessary education, or if there aren't enough assets to balance your lack of earning power or underemployment against your spouse's greater earning power.

When possible, it is always better to receive a distribution of property rather than maintenance. Property settlements are irrevocable. Spousal maintenance is nearly always temporary and generally can be modified, although support in rare circumstances can be stipulated as non-modifiable. Keep in mind that spousal support is taxable to the payee (the person who receives the dollars) and tax deductible to the payer (the person who pays the dollars). This can generate some overall tax savings if the payer is in a higher tax bracket than the payee.

MYTH 4
I have the kids, so I should keep the house

When there are children still living at home, the custodial parent may feel very strongly about keeping the house. The homemaker spouse may have put many hours into the home and have a great deal of pride in it. However, the house can become an expensive tax trap for the unwary.

It is important to consider the cost of maintaining the house, including such items as property taxes, insurance, and ongoing or catch-up maintenance costs. These can be significant, especially in a large and expensive home. The owner spouse may discover that his or her reduced income is no longer adequate to afford to keep the house. In situations where all discretionary income is consumed by the house, an individual can find him or herself trapped in a house which becomes run down over time and harder and harder to sell.

MYTH 5
I'm the mother, so I get custody of the children

It's hardly that black and white. In the past, a mother had to be extremely unfit to lose custody of her children. Now, courts are looking more at whose caretaking is in the best interests of the children. This involves family history, educational needs, time availability of the custodial parent, visitation opportunities, and the wishes of the child. A primary consideration is still who has historically been the primary caregiver. More fathers are petitioning for custody and getting it. Some mothers want to release the major responsibility of child care in order to pursue careers or other interests, and divorce is their opportunity to do this.

Regardless of who the children live with, the most important issue is that both parents stay involved in their children's lives and be equally concerned with what is best for the child. Parenting plans are often difficult and emotional issues to resolve. A family law attorney is a vital source in learning and preserving your rights concerning your children.

MYTH 6
I don't have to worry about health insurance because I'm still covered by my former spouse's plan

After your divorce is final, you can no longer be covered as a spouse under your former spouse's health plan. However, if your spouse's employer has more than 20 employees, they must offer you 36 months of guaranteed continued coverage under federal COBRA laws. You will most likely pay for this out of your own pocket.

In Washington State, effective as of January 1994, one has the right to convert from an ex-spouse's group policy to an individual policy with the same insurer *without proof of insurability* within 90 days of leaving the group plan. Being on COBRA counts as being on the group plan. Any dependent children can continue to be covered under either parent's health insurance plan. Be sure and check the health insurance regulations in your state.

MYTH 7
If my spouse is assigned the debt, I am off the hook

Wrong. If credit card companies cannot collect from your ex-spouse, they legally have the right to come after you for debt incurred during the marriage. Even though the court may order one spouse to pay certain marital debt, the creditor still has the right to collect from either or both spouses.

Consider this: If your ex-spouse files bankruptcy sometime in the future and you were party to the debt, you could find creditors chasing you. The creditor doesn't care who was assigned the debt in the divorce—they just want the money.

MYTH 8
My spouse and I can remain friends

Well, that isn't exactly a myth—it is possible at a price. The price may be that one of you is too nice and doesn't ask for what you are entitled to receive.

Every divorcing couple should be required to rent the movie *War of the Roses*. This movie, while extreme, does provide a humorous view of a complicated process and emotional minefield. It may lead you to agree that the term "civilized divorce," like "jumbo shrimp," is something of an oxymoron.

Chapter One—Divorce Myths And Mysteries

MYTH 9
I'll get more if I get him/her in front of the judge

Perhaps, but it is not guaranteed. It depends on how reasonable your stated needs are. If you are at the point where your last settlement volley has been shot into your spouse's camp or visa versa, it is time to evaluate the potential costs versus the benefits of going before the judge.

Whenever you are at the mercy of a third party to make a judgment on the merits of your situation, you are at risk. Judges bring their own philosophical and legal biases to the bench which can have a big impact on the ultimate outcome of your case. If you are fortunate enough to know which judge will be assigned to your case, your attorney may be familiar with the style and track record of that judge and may be able to advise you on how they might rule on your behalf. However, there are never any guarantees. Remember "a bird in hand…"

MYTH 10
Any attorney can do a good job on my divorce

Don't make this mistake. We've seen some abysmal results by attorneys who didn't know or care enough about economic disparity to suggest appropriate solutions.

You need an attorney who specializes in divorce or whose practice is heavily weighted in that direction. Your attorney also should be a good litigator, just in case you end up in a courtroom. Ask what percentage of his or her cases end up in court and if it is possible to observe him or her in the courtroom. Alternatively, talk to someone whom the attorney represented in a litigated dissolution.

Another way to determine if the attorney you are interviewing might work for you is to ask his/her thoughts on your proposal to split the marital community assets, including both property and income. Be sure you select an attorney who can support your needs fully. And if yours is a long term marriage, seek an attorney who will suggest disparate settlements of property and income in order to come to an equitable conclusion.

CHAPTER TWO
From We To Me Needs

One of the first financial concerns of anyone going through a divorce should be their cash flow. Chances are some aspect of your divorce will have a negative impact on your lifestyle. You may have moved out of the family home and into an apartment, you could be facing large temporary child support payments that need to be met, or you could be an unemployed homemaker trying to get by on a drastically reduced income.

Taming The Cash Flow Crisis

Whatever the situation, you need to calculate your new living expenses and income sources. This is often one of the first things an attorney is going to ask you to do. Keep in mind new expenses that will be (or are being) incurred as a result of changes in your lifestyle. For example, you may have property taxes and mortgage payments due on a new residence, loan costs for a replacement car, attorney fees, college tuition and book costs to improve your job prospects, health insurance costs, child support or alimony to pay, etc.

Hot On The Trail

In order to put together an accurate budget for yourself and your attorney, stay hot on the trail of every dime and dollar you spend. Make sure you include sporadic expenses such as insurance payments, property taxes, and car licenses, as well as new expenses such as health insurance or education costs. Try to minimize your use of cash. Checkbook entries can provide an easy way of tracking costs. If you can't avoid using cash, carry a little notebook so that you can record your purchases. Keep receipts for any major cash purchases. Keeping good expense records is mandatory if you need to justify a level of spousal support to the court or to a mediator.

Separate Your Expenses

If your spouse has not yet left the family home, attempt to separate your daily financial life from his or hers as much as possible. Set up separate bank accounts and leave community assets untouched. An exception to this rule is if you believe your spouse might abscond with all your liquid assets. If this is a possibility, your attorney can advise you of legal means available to "block" accounts and minimize opportunities for a clean-out by your intended ex. You can protect yourself from this by setting up a cash cushion account in your own name and funding it with your share of community cash. Keep good records of any withdrawals you or your spouse makes from community accounts. An alternative is to split the proceeds from one community account between you and your spouse and then close it. This provides each of you with a starting balance.

Curb The Credit Card Risk

While we have devoted a later chapter to the subject of debts, it is worthwhile to state the following more than once: If you are tempted to use community credit cards during the separation but pre-divorce period, don't. Try to obtain a card in your name only and leave the joint accounts alone. Talk to your attorney about this issue. If you absolutely have to use joint credit cards, keep excellent records and be prepared to provide your spouse with copies of statements. Remember that the court, in almost all cases, will require you to pay off post-separation debt yourself.

Bulletproof Your Foundation

As we've already discussed, if you are asking for child support or spousal support, you will need to provide your attorney with your expense needs. Many women and men hurriedly throw together their best guess as to their monthly expenditures and shortchange themselves in the process. Accurate expense records and estimates are very important. We can't stress how important—especially for refugees from long term marriages. Your living expense requirements are one of the biggest factors which will influence your long term financial picture after the divorce is over.

Three Expense Scenarios

There are three expense scenarios you should evaluate: The first is your historical marital lifestyle. Go back to your community records—checkbooks, tax returns, receipt file—and thoroughly compile an expense picture of that period. Don't forget to include items such as vacations, charitable contributions, and savings plans.

The second summarization is your temporary lifestyle—a compilation of expenses incurred during the divorce—a time when you are possibly cash strapped and living at a subsistence level. This compilation is often used to justify requests for temporary maintenance.

The third is the expected new lifestyle you plan to live as soon as the big "D" is finished. This new lifestyle should be very familiar to you as your goal is to replicate as much as possible the manner in which you were living during marriage. In reality, at least for the short term, it is likely that both spouses will need to reduce their standard of living somewhat from that enjoyed during the marriage. After all, the same income and asset dollars now must cover two households instead of just one. There may also be new retraining or college costs if you are economically disadvantaged compared to your spouse.

It is fairly common for one or both spouses to pump up or pad their living expense numbers in an attempt to justify a particular support level or property division. Don't. Padding does more harm than good. Your spouse will know if you are trying to illustrate a higher standard of living than enjoyed during the marriage and will certainly speak up. You are unlikely to gain anything and will only hurt your own credibility. Be completely and scrupulously honest.

Now, use a photocopier to enlarge the following worksheet and make three copies, pick up the pencil and calculator and go to work. Remember, the assets and income awarded at the conclusion of the divorce may have a lot to do with how carefully you've completed this part of your homework.

WORKSHEET 2A

LIVING EXPENSES

Date Compiled: _____ ____Pre-dissolution joint lifestyle expenses
____Temporary interim expenses
____Expected post-dissolution expenses

	Month	Year
Housing		
Rent, if applicable		
Mortgage principal & interest payments		
Installment payments for home equity loans or second mortgages		
Property taxes		
Homeowners insurance		
Maintenance & repair/yard care		
Furniture/appliance replacement		
Total Housing		
Utilities		
Heat (gas & oil)		
Electricity		
Water, sewer, and garbage		
Telephone		
Cable		
Other _____		
Total Utilities		
Food & Supplies		
Food for self		
Household supplies		
Meals eaten out		
Pet Care		
Other _____		
Total Food & Supplies		
Children		
Food for ____ children		
Daycare/baby-sitting		
Clothing		
Tuition if applicable		
Health care		
Other _____		
Other _____		
Total Children's Expenses		

FINANCIAL PLANNING *from* WE *to* ME

	Month	Year
Transportation		
Vehicle payments or leases	_____	_____
Gas, oil, & routine maintenance	_____	_____
Vehicle insurance	_____	_____
Vehicle license	_____	_____
Parking	_____	_____
Other _____	_____	_____
Total Transportation	_____	_____
Health Care (not including children)		
Insurance not paid by employer	_____	_____
Uninsured medical, dental, and eye care expenses	_____	_____
Counseling	_____	_____
Prescription drugs	_____	_____
Other _____	_____	_____
Total Health Care	_____	_____
Personal Expenses (not including children)		
Clothing	_____	_____
Hair care/personal care expenses	_____	_____
Clubs & recreation	_____	_____
Education	_____	_____
Books, magazines, newspapers, & photos	_____	_____
Gifts	_____	_____
Vacation/recreation/entertainment	_____	_____
Other _____	_____	_____
Other _____	_____	_____
Total Personal Expenses	_____	_____
Miscellaneous Expenses		
Life insurance if not paid by employer	_____	_____
Disability insurance	_____	_____
Charitable contributions	_____	_____
Banking/credit fees	_____	_____
Legal/tax/financial advisory fees	_____	_____
Other _____	_____	_____
Other _____	_____	_____
Total Miscellaneous Expenses	_____	_____
Total Household Expenses (total all above)	_____	_____

CHAPTER THREE
Tug Of War

While the picture seems ludicrous, it happens. I've been to court and have watched as children lined up behind one parent. There is nothing sadder than to witness children being encouraged to take sides in a divorce. Pity the poor parent who isn't on the right side. Getting the children to take sides can damage everyone involved. Remember that the conflict between the parents can be more hurtful to the children than the actual separation.

Parenting Plan

Generally, the first priority of parents and the courts is to adopt a just parenting plan for the children. Again, another potential candidate for the oxymoron dictionary—"just parenting plan." Some parents do try to make children a priority by negotiating joint custody deals. They live in the same neighborhood, the children alternate homes, and the parents deal with each other with integrity and fairness. This can work, but in reality it is rare. In Washington State, the 1987 Parenting Act limits any attempt to treat a child like a ping pong ball by requiring a history of shared parenting and reasonable residential proximity before permitting a 50/50 type parenting plan. Sometimes a custody battle ensues. Frequently one parent obtains custody and the other receives visitation rights and pays child support. Therein lies the rub. It is almost impossible to divide fiscal responsibility and time requirements equally between both parents. One usually receives too much of one portion and not enough of the other.

Child Support By The Schedule

Child support is just that—support each parent is ordered to pay toward the care of his or her children. The basic support amount is calculated based on state-by-state devised tables. At the end of this chapter, we have included the Washington State Child Support Schedule. Check with your local court or Bar Association regarding your state's guidelines. Child support is determined primarily by the combined income of both parents. The second element is the age of the child or children in question and the number of children that each parent must support. In the state of Washington, support is usually paid until the child reaches age 18 or graduates from high school, whichever is later.

The base amount of support is proportionately divided between the parents according to their respective levels of net after-tax monthly income. Note that spousal support already ordered is considered to be income to the receiver and a deduction to the income of the payer for purposes of calculating income available for child support. The other expenses that are deducted before determining the amount of income available for support include union dues, industrial insurance premiums, mandatory pension contributions, and normal business expenses.

Special or extraordinary expenses such as health insurance premiums, private school tuition, or daycare costs are proportionately added to this base level. The parent who pays for these extra expenses receives a credit for their payment against his or her total obligation.

The non-custodial parent pays his/her portion of the child support to the custodial parent. This transfer is *not* tax deductible to the payer. Even though the paying parent doesn't get to keep the money, he or she still has to pay taxes on it, and the recipient of the monthly checks receives the children's money as tax-free income. It is possible to categorize a portion of extraordinary child support as alimony/spousal maintenance, which can offer a tax advantage to the support payer, as long as the net after tax transfer payment to the recipient remains the same as the amount of the mandated support amount if paid as child support. Child support payments cannot be discharged in bankruptcy. This can include an assigned obligation to pay a child's medical bills or other necessary expenses.

Tinkering With The Formulas

Although there are child support guidelines in all states, attorneys and judges may request or mandate adjustments in child support awards in accordance with individual circumstances. In Washington State, adjustments are rarely allowed below the scheduled amount unless under exceptional circumstances which fall within the statute.

After a child support order is issued, a court may modify the order in a variety of circumstances with regard to future payments. Typically this occurs when the child moves into the next age bracket or if there has been a substantial change of circumstances. Be aware that the allocation of residential time may impact the child support paid by the non-custodial spouse. In Washington State, for example, child support may be reduced when the non-custodial spouse has the children for a significant amount of time. Ask your attorney about the rules in your state.

The College Dilemma

College costs are not considered a mandatory obligation of either parent. However, in Washington State the court can order parents to pay college or other post-secondary school expenses in appropriate circumstances. This issue is often a factor in settlement negotiations, and the cost can be allocated in various ways between the parents and the child. For instance, the parents could agree to split the college costs based on their proportional income. If the father earns $50,000 and the mother earns $30,000, then he would pay 62.5% of costs and she 37.5%. Although this is not child support, it is enforceable in the same manner as any court order.

One way to solve this problem so that the custodial parent is not burdened with all the post-majority expenses is to take some of the marital assets at the time of the divorce and establish a trust for the benefit of the child(ren). In this way the child(ren)'s post-majority expenses (away at school or at home), including college tuition, books, and so forth, will be paid for by both parents. If the property is to be split in an unequal percentage, then the contribution to the trust should also be pro rata. As the court will not require parents to contribute to such a trust, it must be a voluntary arrangement worked out by both parties.

In certain circumstances, the court can require post-majority support to help a child who has mental or physical disabilities.

Juggling Tax Exemptions

One of you will be able to deduct the child(ren) on your federal income tax return. The question is who? The current IRS rule is for the custodial parent to receive the exemption(s) on the basis that the child support calculated between both parents almost never covers all the expenses of raising a child.

The parent with the higher taxable income will receive the most tax relief from the use of the exemptions. One plus—even if the custodial parent gives up all of the children's personal exemptions, he or she can still file his or her income tax return as a head of household rather than under the higher single rates. If there is more than one child, the exemptions can be alternated between the two parents in some fashion. However, if the higher earning spouse's income exceeds an IRS imposed ceiling, the amount of personal exemptions that he or she can deduct is gradually reduced until it is gone. In this case, the exemptions may be more beneficial in the hands of the lower-tax-bracket spouse. The exemptions will automatically go to the custodial parent unless they are assigned to the other parent as part of the divorce settlement.

We recommend the custodial parent request to keep the exemptions and consider giving one or more exemptions to the non-custodial parent on an every-other-year rotation or sporadically as a way of encouraging the non-custodial parent to pay child support. The custodial parent would be required to sign IRS form 8332 for the non-custodial parent to file in each year that the exemption is released to the non-custodial parent.

Child Support Worksheets

On the following pages we have duplicated the standard Washington State child support calculation worksheet and economic table. Your state's form may, of course, be different. Your attorney generally will complete this form and obtain the court order for the child support. These worksheets can serve as a guide as you gather the necessary information for your attorney. Keep in mind that the court can and often does deviate from these guidelines in setting child support amounts within certain statutory limits.

The family of Sam and Sally Smith illustrates a typical child support calculation as required for their two children, ages 13 and 8.

Sam:	Monthly Salary:	$8,000
	Income Taxes Withheld:	$2,500
	FICA Taxes Withheld:	$433
	Mandatory Pension Contrib.	$480
Sally:	Monthly Salary	$1,000
	Spousal Maintenance	$1,500
	Income Taxes Withheld:	$375
	FICA Taxes Withheld:	$77
	Union Dues	$20

Sam pays an extra $50 per month to cover the children under his health care plan, while Sally pays $100 per month for after-school day care for their youngest child.

Chapter Three—Tug Of War

EXAMPLE 3A
SAM AND SALLY SMITH

Name and Age of Children: Steve 13 and Susan 8

MONTHLY GROSS INCOME	HUSB	WIFE
1. Wages/Salary	$8,000.00	$1,000.00
2. Net Business Income		
3. Spousal Support		$1,500.00
4. Rental Income		
5. Interest Income		
6. Other Income		
7. TOTAL GROSS INCOME (Lines 1-6)	$8,000.00	$2,500.00
DEDUCTIONS		
8. Federal Income Tax	$2,500.00	$375.00
9. FICA/Medicare Taxes	$433.00	$76.50
10. Mandatory Union Dues		$20.00
11. Mandatory Pension Contributions	$480.00	
12. Spousal Support	$1,500.00	
13. State Industrial Insurance		
14. TOTAL EXPENSES (Lines 8-13)	$4,913.00	$471.50
15. NET INCOME AVAILABLE FOR SUPPORT (Lines 7 less Line 14)	$3,087.00	$2,028.50
16. TOTAL COMBINED INCOME AVAILABLE FOR SUPPORT	$5,115.50	
17. PROPORTION OF TOTAL INCOME PER PARENT (Line 15 for each divided by Line 16)	60.35%	39.65%

18. BASE CHILD SUPPORT PER ECONOMIC TABLE

    A. Child 1 Steve - $720

    B. Child 2 Susan - $584

FINANCIAL PLANNING *from* WE *to* ME

	HUSB	WIFE
C. Child 3 _____		
D. Child 4 _____		
19. TOTAL OF LINES 18 (A-D): $1,304.00		
20. SUPPORT TO BE PROVIDED BY EACH PARENT: (Line 19 times each parent's Line 17)	$786.91	$517.09
ADJUSTMENTS TO SUPPORT		
21. Health Insurance Paid	$50.00	
22. Extraordinary Health Expenses		
23. Day Care Expenses		$100.00
24. Educational Expenses (non-college)		
25. TOTAL ADJUSTMENTS (Lines 21-24)	$50.00	$100.00
26. FINAL SUPPORT TO BE PROVIDED (includes basic support plus adjustments to support for each parent's extra expenses: (Line 19 plus both parent's Line 25).		$1,454.00
27. FINAL SUPPORT TO BE PROVIDED BY EACH PARENT (Line 26 times each parent's line 17).	$877.43	$576.57
CHILD SUPPORT CREDITS FOR EXTRA EXPENSES: (same amounts as in Line 21-24 above)		
28. Health Insurance paid	$50.00	
29. Extraordinary Health Expenses		
30. Daycare Expenses		$100.00
31. Educational Expenses (non-college)		
32. NET SUPPORT OBLIGATION OF PARENT: Line 27 less lines 28-31).	$827.43	$476.57
33. TRANSFER PAYMENT TO CUSTODIAL PARENT (Line 32 for non-custodial parent equals transfer payment).	$827.43	

WORKSHEET 3A

CHILD SUPPORT CALCULATION

Case I.D.: _____

Name and Age of Children: _____

MONTHLY GROSS INCOME	HUSB	WIFE
1. Wages/Salary	_____	_____
2. Net Business Income	_____	_____
3. Spousal Support	_____	_____
4. Rental Income	_____	_____
5. Interest Income	_____	_____
6. Other Income	_____	_____
7. TOTAL GROSS INCOME (Lines 1-6)	======	======
DEDUCTIONS		
8. Federal Income Tax	_____	_____
9. FICA/Medicare Taxes	_____	_____
10. Mandatory Union Dues	_____	_____
11. Mandatory Pension Contributions	_____	_____
12. Spousal Support	_____	_____
13. State Industrial Insurance	_____	_____
14. TOTAL EXPENSES (Lines 8-13)	======	======
15. NET INCOME AVAILABLE FOR SUPPORT (Lines 7 less Line 14)	_____	_____
16. TOTAL COMBINED INCOME AVAILABLE FOR SUPPORT	_____	_____
17. PROPORTION OF TOTAL INCOME PER PARENT (Line 15 for each divided by Line 16)	======	======
18. BASE CHILD SUPPORT PER ECONOMIC TABLE		

    A. Child 1 _____

FINANCIAL PLANNING *from* WE *to* ME

	HUSB	WIFE

B. Child 2 _____

C. Child 3 _____

D. Child 4 _____

19. TOTAL OF LINES 18 (A-D)

20. SUPPORT TO BE PROVIDED BY EACH PARENT: (Line 19 times each parent's Line 17)

ADJUSTMENTS TO SUPPORT

21. Health Insurance Paid

22. Extraordinary Health Expenses

23. Day Care Expenses

24. Educational Expenses (non-college)

25. TOTAL ADJUSTMENTS (Lines 21-24)

26. FINAL SUPPORT TO BE PROVIDED (includes basic support plus adjustments to support for each parent's extra expenses: (Line 19 plus both parent's Line 25).

27. FINAL SUPPORT TO BE PROVIDED BY EACH PARENT (Line 26 times each parent's line 17).

CHILD SUPPORT CREDITS FOR EXTRA EXPENSES: (same amounts as in Line 21-24 above)

28. Health Insurance paid

29. Extraordinary Health Expenses

30. Daycare Expenses

31. Educational Expenses (non-college)

32. NET SUPPORT OBLIGATION OF PARENT: Line 27 less lines 28-31).

33. TRANSFER PAYMENT TO CUSTODIAL PARENT (Line 32 for non-custodial parent equals transfer payment).

Chapter Three—Tug Of War

Economic Table
Monthly Basic Support Obligation Per Child
(KEY: A = AGE 0-11 B = AGE 12-18)

Combined Monthly Net Income	One Child Family A	One Child Family B	Two Children Family A	Two Children Family B	Three Children Family A	Three Children Family B	Four Children Family A	Four Children Family B	Five Children Family A	Five Children Family B
	For income less than $600, refer to Standards for Establishing Lower and Upper Limits on Child Support Amounts, #2: Income below six hundred dollars. (See page 2)									
600	133	164	103	127	86	106	73	90	63	78
700	155	191	120	148	100	124	85	105	74	91
800	177	218	137	170	115	142	97	120	84	104
900	199	246	154	191	129	159	109	135	95	118
1000	220	272	171	211	143	177	121	149	105	130
1100	242	299	188	232	157	194	133	164	116	143
1200	264	326	205	253	171	211	144	179	126	156
1300	285	352	221	274	185	228	156	193	136	168
1400	307	379	238	294	199	246	168	208	147	181
1500	327	404	254	313	212	262	179	221	156	193
1600	347	428	269	333	225	278	190	235	166	205
1700	367	453	285	352	238	294	201	248	175	217
1800	387	478	300	371	251	310	212	262	185	228
1900	407	503	316	390	264	326	223	275	194	240
2000	427	527	331	409	277	342	234	289	204	252
2100	447	552	347	429	289	358	245	303	213	264
2200	467	577	362	448	302	374	256	316	223	276
2300	487	601	378	467	315	390	267	330	233	288
2400	506	626	393	486	328	406	278	343	242	299
2500	526	650	408	505	341	421	288	356	251	311
2600	534	661	416	513	346	428	293	362	256	316
2700	542	670	421	520	351	435	298	368	259	321
2800	549	679	427	527	356	440	301	372	262	324
2900	556	686	431	533	360	445	305	376	266	328
3000	561	693	436	538	364	449	308	380	268	331
3100	566	699	439	543	367	453	310	383	270	334
3200	569	704	442	546	369	457	312	386	272	336
3300	573	708	445	549	371	459	314	388	273	339
3400	574	710	446	551	372	460	315	389	274	340
3500	575	711	447	552	373	461	316	390	275	341
3600	577	712	448	553	374	462	317	391	276	342
3700	578	713	449	554	375	463	318	392	277	343
3800	581	719	452	558	377	466	319	394	278	344
3900	596	736	463	572	386	477	326	404	284	352
4000	609	753	473	584	395	488	334	413	291	360
4100	623	770	484	598	404	500	341	422	298	368
4200	638	788	495	611	413	511	350	431	305	377
4300	651	805	506	625	422	522	357	441	311	385
4400	664	821	516	637	431	532	364	449	317	392
4500	677	836	525	649	438	542	371	458	323	400
4600	689	851	535	661	446	552	377	467	329	407
4700	701	866	545	673	455	562	384	475	335	414
4800	713	882	554	685	463	572	391	483	341	422
4900	726	897	564	697	470	581	398	491	347	429
5000	738	912	574	708	479	592	404	500	353	437
	For income greater than $5,000, refer to Standards for Establishing Lower and Upper Limits on Child Support Amounts, #3: Income above five thousand and seven thousand dollars. (See page 3)									
5100	751	928	584	720	487	602	411	509	359	443
5200	763	943	593	732	494	611	418	517	365	451
5300	776	959	602	744	503	621	425	525	371	458
5400	788	974	612	756	511	632	432	533	377	466
5500	800	989	622	768	518	641	439	542	383	473
5600	812	1004	632	779	527	651	446	551	389	480
5700	825	1019	641	791	535	661	452	559	395	488
5800	837	1035	650	803	543	671	459	567	401	495
5900	850	1050	660	815	551	681	466	575	407	502
6000	862	1065	670	827	559	691	473	584	413	509
6100	875	1081	680	839	567	701	479	593	418	517
6200	887	1096	689	851	575	710	486	601	424	524
6300	899	1112	699	863	583	721	493	609	430	532
6400	911	1127	709	875	591	731	500	617	436	539
6500	924	1142	718	887	599	740	506	626	442	546
6600	936	1157	728	899	607	750	513	635	448	554
6700	949	1172	737	911	615	761	520	643	454	561
6800	961	1188	747	923	623	770	527	651	460	568
6900	974	1203	757	935	631	780	533	659	466	575
7000	986	1218	767	946	639	790	540	668	472	583

For income greater than $7,000, refer to Standards for Establishing Lower and Upper Limits on Child Support Amounts, #3: Income above five thousand and seven thousand dollars.

CHAPTER FOUR
Income Sharing

Yes, it does happen. You or your spouse may be required to pay spousal support known also as maintenance or alimony. All too often one spouse is cash flow poor and the other cash flow rich, relatively speaking. In cases like this, spousal support may be just the answer. The need for income sharing is generally supported by facts relating to an earning disparity between the spouses, the length of the marriage, the needs of the lower earning spouse, and his or her ability to increase his or her income over time or simply to be productively employed. Spousal support is not an automatic right. Many settlements do not include any form of spousal support at all. And unlike our picture, spousal support can be paid from women to men just as easily if the woman's earnings exceed the man's and economic disparity is evident.

The Case For Support

In short term marriages (five years or less) or where both spouses have established careers, spousal support is rare. It is most frequently found in divorces involving long term marriages where one spouse has remained at home or let his or her career take a back seat to the primary earner's.

Retraining Options

Factors in retraining/education of the disadvantaged spouse include such issues as age, previous education and/or employment, and both mental and physical health. It is not realistic to expect a 55 year old woman with little or no education or training and limited work experience to pop right into the workforce and make a livable wage. On the other hand, a 40-year-old woman who has been out of the workforce while raising a family could be expected to pursue retraining or a college degree with the intent of eventually contributing to her own support.

Caution—even in long term marriages, spousal support is rarely awarded for a lifetime. Most awards are for short periods of readjustment or retraining and are intended to help the individual reestablish his or her place in the working world. In a few cases, long term maintenance is required to develop an equitable solution to an asset poor but income rich marriage. In any case, maintenance always terminates at the death of either the payer or the payee.

IRS Supplied Pain Pill

Spousal support, as far as the IRS is concerned, is a transfer of income from the payer to the payee. Taxes are paid by the

Chapter Four—Income Sharing

payee, and the court-ordered income transfer is fully tax deductible to the payer. This can offer significant tax planning advantages for both parties if the payer is in a high tax bracket while the payee is in a lower one. As illustrated in the examples at the end of this chapter, the actual after-tax cost of maintenance may be much less to the payer than it first appears, easing the pain of writing those support checks.

You should be aware that money transferred from one spouse to another does not qualify as a deduction to the payer unless the spouses file separate tax returns, are under a decree of separation or divorce, and are not members of the same household when payment is made. Further, the payer and payee may jointly agree in writing that alimony/spousal support will not be deductible to one nor taxable to the other. This election can be made annually if it was provided for in the divorce decree. Any such election made should be attached to each party's tax return.

Excessive manipulation of asset transfers through tax deductible maintenance payments has been severely curtailed under current laws dealing with excess "front loading." The intent of these rules is to keep a high income payer from disguising property division as spousal support in order to take advantage of the tax deduction.

If the total alimony payment in year one is greater than the average of the total payments in years two and three by more than $15,000, the excess must be included by the payer in his/her taxable income and is not taxable to payee. This is recaptured in the third year. The same problem will occur if payments in year two are greater than payments in year three by more than $15,000. The formula to calculate excessive support is complicated. If you want a detailed understanding of this area, you will find instructions, examples, and a worksheet in IRS Publication 504.

Generally, courts are reluctant to award total combined child support and alimony of more than one-half the net income of the support payer, even when the payee spouse needs every dime she/he can get. This is an area for negotiation by the spouses and their attorneys. Generally a court will not force one marriage partner to tap personal assets to support the other. Instead, some form of income production would be the source of the maintenance dollars.

IRA Contributions

One welcome benefit of spousal support paid over a period of time is that it can be used to make a deposit into an Individual Retirement Account (IRA) even if one is not employed. Could it be that the Internal Revenue Service is aware of the fact that spousal support is just payment for one's contribution to the marital economic unit? We think so.

Co-Habitation Or Remarriage Issues

Most support stops upon remarriage. Some support may stop if you live with another person. It is possible, though, to agree to have your support deemed as non-modifiable upon remarriage or cohabitation. It is also possible to agree that support can be reviewed upon remarriage based on the economic circumstances rather than terminating automatically. Cohabitation by the lower earning spouse during the divorce process can reduce or eliminate an award of spouse maintenance at the court's discretion.

Alimony Trusts

So you don't want the way you run your personal life to govern whether or not you receive the agreed upon amount of spousal support—there is another alternative—the alimony trust. The major difference between this mode of receiving your support dollars and the pay-as-you-go mode is that dollars transferred to an "alimony trust" are not deductible to the grantor or taxable to the recipient. The income from an alimony trust is treated for tax purposes as trust income; therefore, it does not qualify under the special rule that allows alimony dollars to be contributed to an IRA. If the beneficiary of an alimony trust should die prior to consuming the trust principal, it is possible to have it revert back to the grantor.

Loose Ends

Spousal support in the State of Washington is generally a fixed amount paid over a period of years. Often, the amount decreases after an initial period. For example, the court may decide that a spouse will receive $3,000/month for 36 months, $2,500 for the next 24 months, and $2,000 for the last 12 months. Ideally support dollars paid over a period of time would be adjusted by a cost of living adjustment to ward off the impact of inflation on the payments. This doesn't usually happen.

Lastly, one should consider what would happen to the support income if the payer should become disabled or die. You should, if the payer is insurable, put a term life policy on his or her life or take over an existing policy for an amount adequate to completely fund your spousal support. The need for life insurance is also discussed in Chapter Twelve. Insuring your support against disability is more difficult. Disability insurance is difficult to get—one must be in almost perfect health, and it is not inexpensive. This is an area to discuss with your attorney. He or she should help you decide on whether it is appropriate for you or your spouse to pay the protection dollar for insurance on spousal support. Get a commitment before the ink on the decree is dry.

EXAMPLE 4A

A SPOONFUL OF SUGAR
HELPS THE MEDICINE GO DOWN

JOHN

Annual Income	$100,000
Filing Status	Single
Number of Exemptions	One
Spousal Support Proposed	$24,000
Marginal Tax Bracket before Spousal Support	31%
Marginal Tax Bracket after Spousal Support	31%
Net after tax cost of Spousal Support	$16,560

SUSAN

Annual Income	$10,000
Filing Status	Head of Household
Gross Spousal Support Proposed	$24,000
Marginal Tax Bracket before Spousal Support	15%
Marginal Tax Bracket after Spousal Support	15%
Net after tax benefit of Spousal Support	$20,400

EXAMPLE 4B

SAM

Annual Income	$70,000
Filing Status	Single
Number of Exemptions	One
Spousal Support Proposed	$12,000
Marginal Tax Bracket before Spousal Support	31%
Marginal Tax Bracket after Spousal Support	28%
Net after tax cost of Spousal Support	$8,280

SALLY

Annual Income	$15,000
Filing Status	Single
Gross Spousal Support Proposed	$12,000
Marginal Tax Bracket before Spousal Support	15%
Marginal Tax Bracket after Spousal Support	15%
Net after tax benefit of Spousal Support	$10,200

CHAPTER FIVE
Slicing The Marital Pie

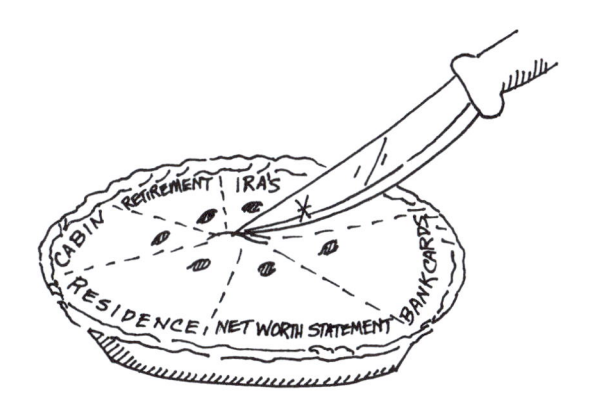

In other words, what assets will be sliced and how big will the slices be? Before one can start dividing assets, one must determine which items are truly marital property.

Mine, Yours, Ours

In some states this is easily determined. For example, in the State of Washington, nearly everything acquired during the marriage is community property. The other community property states are Arizona, California, Idaho, Louisiana, Nevada, New Mexico, Texas, and Wisconsin. The basic principle of Washington's community property laws is that a husband and wife contribute equally to the marital community whether or not both work outside the home. Therefore, any money earned by either spouse during the marriage is community property that belongs equally to both. This includes not only salary earned but also benefits such as 401(k) and pension plans, sick pay, etc. Separate property is property owned by either spouse prior to the marriage, or received as a gift or inheritance, and any increase in its value remains separate absent a written agreement to the contrary. In other states, it will depend on state law. Other states may use an equitable division of property derived from the common law system for the marital property. Separate assets may remain separate, but in some cases the appreciation of such may be deemed to be joint property. Only Mississippi follows traditional common law principles, dividing property according to who has legal title to it. See Chapter Six for a more detailed discussion of separate property. Discuss your state's laws with your attorney.

For the sake of this discussion, we shall assume that all of the items listed below are marital assets, and thus joint property.

Typical Marital Assets

- Residence
- Real estate purchased with community funds
- Business value, including goodwill
- Bank accounts
- Investment accounts
- IRA accounts
- 401k/403b plan accounts
- Defined benefit pension plans, profit sharing, employee stock ownership programs, etc.

Chapter Five—Slicing The Marital Pie

- Accumulated vacation and sick pay
- Cash value life insurance policies
- Autos, boats, furnishings, and other personal property

This list is by no means comprehensive. If you acquired property during the marriage, it is probably community property unless you have inherited or been gifted separate funds. Your attorney can assist you in reviewing your situation and helping you get started compiling the asset information in your particular situation.

Business Difficulties

If a business is part of the marital financial pie, it can substantially complicate the property division. Frequently this has been the "cash cow" for the marriage. If one spouse is the principal operator, the business will generally be awarded to that spouse with other assets going to the non-operator spouse. The valuation of a business can be difficult and usually requires an expert such as a business valuation specialist or accountant. Many businesses have a certain measure of goodwill that has value, but this is difficult to pin down without expert assistance. It is nearly always worth the cost to hire a specialist to value the business, as a successful firm can be worth a considerable sum of money.

When the business is a major marital asset, it may prove impossible to completely compensate the non-operator spouse using other assets. In this case, some form of note from the business owner spouse secured by the business or other real assets may be necessary. If possible, consider getting the loan through a commercial lender. This gives the non-operator spouse a lump sum payment instead of monthly installments and eliminates the default risk associated with a personal note.

A business owner's cash flow merits extra scrutiny due to his or her ability to use depreciation and personal expenses disguised as business expenses to reduce the taxable business income without really reducing the actual cash flow or impacting the business owner's lifestyle. An accountant or similar business valuation specialist can be of great assistance here.

Invisible Assets

Another item with value is a degree or license earned or awarded during the marriage, if it relates directly to the earning power of one of the parties. This is particularly clear when one spouse deferred his or her educational efforts to support the other spouse's attainment of credentials. This action often results in an opportunity cost to one spouse and increased earnings potential for the other. Courts increasingly take into account the cost to the community of the lost income while one spouse attended school, the actual tuition costs and perhaps the opportunity cost to the lower earning spouse. Although future earnings per se are not categorized as an asset of the marital union, they can be a factor in obtaining a fair division of the assets and in the awarding of spousal support.

Social Security is another asset which may favor one spouse over the other due to disparity in earning power. This is particularly bothersome in long term marriages where the wife maintained the home and the husband got credit for wages. His Social Security benefit will be twice that of his stay-at-home spouse. Even if both spouses worked, one still may have a greater benefit if he or she earned considerably more than his or her spouse.

Mystery Assets

Hidden assets may be a problem area for the partner who has deferred responsibility of finances to the other. A good place to check for mystery assets is your most recent joint tax return or your spouse's return if you filed separately. If you earned more than $400 in interest during the year, all income producing accounts must be listed on schedule B. Check for unfamiliar accounts with income reported. If your spouse is a key employee or officer of a company you may also wish to check with his or her employer for deferred compensation contracts or stock options that could be worth a considerable sum in the future. This is like digging for gold—you may uncover money in accounts of which you were not even aware. I'm constantly surprised at how many wives feel their husbands may be hiding assets. Generally this turns out not to be true, but the suspicion is fostered by lack of full sharing of financial information between martial partners.

If you suspect big secrets are hidden, get a forensic accountant involved. Such professionals are experts at following income and tax trails to exotic hiding places such as offshore trusts or bank accounts in Switzerland and are very expensive to hire—so be sure of the need first.

Don't Forget The Pension

Another large asset in many marriages is the future pension benefit earned by one or both spouses through an employer or union. This type of pension is called a defined benefit plan—a plan which promises to pay a monthly benefit to the plan participant upon retirement. Generally the benefit is calculated based on a formula that includes years of service and the employee's average final or career earnings. Every pension plan has its own formula and rules which are discussed in a later chapter.

It is vital that you obtain professional financial assistance in valuing a pension plan benefit. These future benefits can be given a current (today's) dollar value called a present value, but the calculations are fairly complex and can vary greatly depending on the rules of the particular pension plan. Ask your attorney for a referral to a qualified actuary, accountant, or financial planner with experience in performing present value pension valuations.

House Trap Doors

Another area that is usually a mystery to divorcing spouses is the true value of the house. Sure, you can get several free market analyses from realtors or hire a professional appraiser, but that is only part of the story. Just about everyone's home has some degree of deferred gain upon which taxes will be paid when the home is sold. This information must be unearthed so that the true tax and cost of sale adjusted value of the home is evident. See Chapter Eight for more information on this topic.

A Word On Taxes

Transfer of property between spouses incident to a divorce is not a taxable activity if it occurs within two years of the divorce or is related to the ending of marriage. To qualify as relating to the ending of the marriage, the transfer needs to occur within six years of the divorce action and be ordered within the divorce or separation decree.

It behooves you to stop and take a deep breath as you consider which assets are the "most worthy" to own on an after-tax basis. For example, consider the case of Susan and Sam. They own a piece of real estate with a market value of $200,000. They purchased the land 20 years ago and paid only $50,000 for it. They also have a stock portfolio worth $200,000 which they bought over a period of years for a total cost of $120,000. The question we pose to you is, "Which asset should Susan ask for?" Clue: Which one has the smallest difference between purchase price and today's market value?

	Real Estate	Stock Portfolio
Current Value	$200,000	$200,000
Less Cost Basis	50,000	120,000
Equals Taxable Gain	$150,000	$80,000
Tax Due on Gain	42,000	22,400
Current Value	$200,000	$200,000
Less Deferred Capital Gains Tax	42,000	22,400
Net After Tax Value of Asset	$158,000	$177,600

As you can see, deferred taxes can make a big difference in the actual value of an asset. Always check the tax consequences of all of the assets to be divided. It is also important to get the cost basis records for each asset into the hands of the spouse who receives it at the time of separation. That way, when the asset is finally sold, the seller does not have to come begging to an ex-spouse for paperwork that may have long since vanished.

An Exception To Tax-Free Transfers

Series EE Bonds are the one asset which does not enjoy tax free transfer status. Instead, Series EE bonds transferred incident to a divorce are taxable to the person transferring ownership. The deferred interest earned over the years these bonds have been owned must be reported to the IRS as taxable income in the year of the transfer.

Drafting Your Game Plan

Use the following worksheet to summarize your assets (exclude earned income). Where possible, back up all values with investment statements or references to sources and dates of valuation. You may wish to fill out one worksheet with values as of the date of separation and another with current values. Depending on the nature of a particular asset, your attorney and financial advisor may need to have both a current value and the value on your date of separation for some assets such as retirement programs so they may accurately credit you and/or your spouse for post-separation payments or contributions.

For ease of use, enlarge the worksheet on a copier and make enough copies to list all your assets on two lists: 1) value at date of separation for all marital assets, and 2) value as close to anticipated date of divorce as possible. Refer to our earlier list of typical marital assets for assistance. Go through your tax returns and filing cabinets to pick up those forgotten investments or accounts. Look around the house and yard for any personal assets that have particular value. List everything you can think of—you can always cross it off later.

WORKSHEET 5A

JOINT ASSETS OF:_____

	Assets	Value Net of Debt	Date & Source of Data	Cost Basis	Allocate Husband	Allocate Wife
1						
2						
3						
4						
5						
6						
7						
8						
9						
10						
11						

* Cost Basis for most assets is the original cost of the property plus the value of any improvements,. Residences have special rules - see chapter eight for more information.

CHAPTER SIX
My Mom Gave It To Me

You may feel that certain assets belong to you alone, and you may be correct. Maybe your mom gave you those particular assets and since then, you've kept them in a separate "cookie jar." If you have done a good job of keeping them separate from martial assets, those assets should not be listed as part of the community property. These assets generally fall into the following categories:

- Property or assets owned before the marriage and kept separate.

- Inheritances kept separate.

- Gifts kept separate.

Marital Unless Proven Otherwise

The assumption in Washington State is that assets are community. If you have separate property that has been commingled with community assets, your attorney can assist you with the research needed to trace and prove the value of the separate contribution.

Documenting the trail of separate dollars through one or more community assets can be difficult and time consuming. However, it may be worth spending the time and effort if you brought a substantial separate asset into the community pot at some point.

Tainting Separate Assets

Common ways separate property can be tainted are when community deposits are made into separate accounts such as brokerage, bank, or mutual funds.

This type of problem can also occur if a community asset or income stream was used to improve a separate asset. Real estate is the most logical asset where this can easily occur. In this situation, the separate property has been tainted and perhaps converted to a community asset. One of the spouses will have to supply facts if he/she wants to return separate and community property to its original characterization. The marital community would be entitled to some form of reimbursement for its contribution to the separate property—possibly a share in its appreciation in value.

As an example, what if one spouse receives some cash as an inheritance and the couple used it to remodel their home. That separate asset has added value to a community asset but is now much more difficult to recover. Another common situation where this can come up is if one spouse owned a separate home

Chapter Six—My Mom Gave It To Me

before the marriage which was sold, and the proceeds were then used as the down payment on a first home of the community. In both of these examples, good records and some dedicated backtracking of dollars is vital if the shorted spouse is to receive any credit for those separate assets in a dissolution.

FINANCIAL PLANNING *from* WE *to* ME

WORKSHEET 6A

SEPARATE ASSETS OF _____

	Asset Description	Value Net of Debt	Date & Source of Data	Cost Basis	Marital Contribution Dollars
1					
2					
3					
4					
5					
6					
7					
8					
9					
10					

* Cost Basis for most assets is the original cost of the property plus the value of any improvements,. Residences have special rules - see chapter eight for more information.

CHAPTER SEVEN
Marital Debts And Other Liabilities

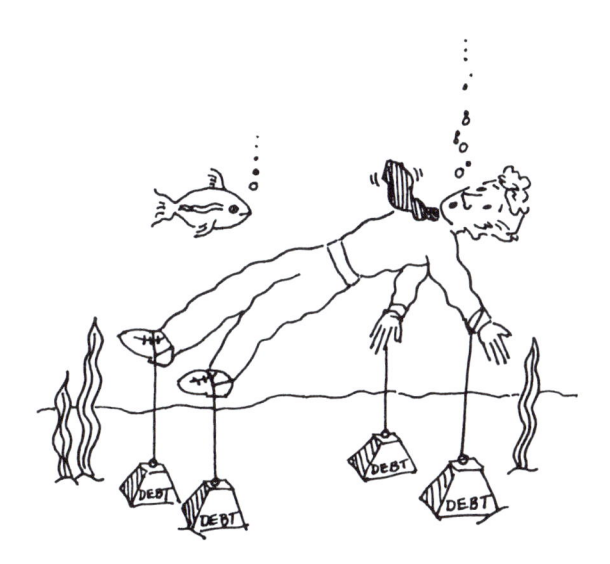

Too bad one can't wave a magic wand and abolish all the debt that is usually associated with assets. Generally, the biggest dilemma with debt revolves around who should be left with it. If no one volunteers, the debt may default into the lap of the larger income earner. Regardless of how you divide it, too much debt can be debilitating.

Common Debts

- Mortgages on community real estate
- Auto loans, boat loans, etc.

- Credit card balances for purchases made during the marriage
- Loans from 401(k) plans
- Loans on life insurance policies
- Family notes

Helpful Hints On Marital Debts

Secured debts generally will follow the assets with which they are secured. So, if you get the house, you also take the mortgage. If your spouse gets the Jaguar, he or she also takes the bank loan associated with it. If the soon-to-be ex's 401(k) has a loan against it, that debt is assigned to him or her. If your insurance policy has been borrowed against, you keep the liability. The reason for this logic is simple. Consider the difficulty if one spouse took the car and the other took the loan. What happens if the loan defaults? The innocent spouse could end up having the auto repossessed. If a debt is in the name of only Spouse A, it is best for that spouse to retain the debt in a split to avoid possible stains on his or her credit record if Spouse B failed to make timely payments.

Unsecured debts—if possible pay these off during the divorce or as part of the final settlement and close the accounts. Just because the VISA bill was assigned to Spouse A doesn't mean that VISA can't or won't come after Spouse B if Spouse A doesn't pay it. The creditor doesn't care who was officially assigned to pay the debt—they can legally hold both parties responsible if both were initial parties to the debt. Should this happen and if the court had ordered Spouse A to pay that particular creditor, Spouse B would have a right to be reimbursed by his or her former spouse if he or she pays the bill. However, you can bet that if VISA can't collect from your ex-spouse, your odds on seeing the money probably aren't all that good either.

Chapter Seven—Marital Debts And Other Liabilities

There is only one safe way to transfer consumer debt from one spouse to the other. Have the paying spouse take out a new card account or credit line in his or her name only and use the proceeds to pay off and close the old joint credit line.

A similar problem can occur with mortgages. Even though Spouse A is assigned the mortgage and Spouse B signs a quit claim deed, if both of your names are on the mortgage, late or missed payments by Spouse A can affect Spouse B's credit rating. Discuss this with your mortgage company—they may be willing to change the mortgage to the mortgage payer's name if they have good income sources. Refinancing the mortgage in a certain number of years is another possibility.

Not as easily quantified, but still important, are the future tax liabilities and cost of selling real estate, any deferred capital gains tax due on investment assets or property, and the deferred income taxes on IRAs and other qualified plans. While these are not current liabilities, they will be in the future and should be taken into consideration when deciding which assets are most desirable to attempt to retain.

In most states, if you plan on selling the family residence or other real estate "imminently" after the dissolution, the cost of the sale as well as the tax due upon sale should be netted from its value when you complete your property list. Just treat those costs as a liability to the property. This forces your spouse to share in the costs of selling the property. The guidelines on this issue differ from county to county and from state to state—so be sure and discuss your court's definition with your attorney.

Credit Card Traps

Try not to use joint credit cards. If you must use them, discuss this activity with your attorney. If you can, open a new account to begin to establish credit in your name alone before

FINANCIAL PLANNING *from* WE *to* ME

you separate. The lower income spouse may find it difficult to get his/her own card once the credit card company is aware of the impending change in marital status and income. If you have or obtain a card, be wary of running up a big balance, as you will eventually have to face paying it off.

If one spouse is making payments on marital credit card balances, keep track of the payments made so that they can be considered in the property division. Once you are separated, inform creditors of the pending divorce. In most states, both spouses are liable for joint credit cards. Close the joint accounts as soon as you can and return any credit cards. Don't just ask for your name to be taken off. Not enough. In Washington State, the creditor can assume that the charging spouse is still acting on behalf of the non-charging spouse until the creditor is notified in writing. Write to all your credit card companies regarding your situation and ask them to send statement copies to each of you so that you can monitor each other's charge activity. The only sure method of ensuring that you are not liable for future charges on a joint credit line is to close it completely. As soon as possible, ask them in writing to close the account and keep a copy of the letter for your records.

If you think that your spouse may not pay a debt, you may want to consider taking the debt in the property division. That way you can receive offsetting property as well, instead of getting a surprise package dumped in your lap in a few months after the divorce.

To clarify the seriousness of the issue, here's a little homework for you:

Call all of your major credit card carriers. Ask them who is responsible for debt incurred on a joint credit card during time of separation but pre-divorce. Ask if you would be responsible

Chapter Seven—Marital Debts And Other Liabilities

for debt incurred by your spouse during this period if he or she did not make his or her share of the payments.

Ask what you should do to protect yourself from being responsible. The answer may vary to some degree from what we've stated above, and you should follow their instructions to the letter.

General Cautions

Try to avoid unsecured notes from one spouse to another when dividing assets. Bankruptcy filing might wipe out this debt with no recourse to the spouse carrying the debt. If you need to have some form of note to balance the property division, attempt to secure it with a piece of real property, preferably one that you would be first in line to foreclose upon in case of bankruptcy. Unfortunately, it won't always be possible to have a secured note when a note from one spouse to the other is necessary to balance the assets.

During or immediately after the divorce obtain a copy of your credit record, which will show you which cards remain open in your name. This can act as a double check to ensure that you have closed as many joint accounts as possible. It is a good idea to check your credit rating periodically. If an unfair blot appears on your credit record due to the actions of an ex-spouse, put a statement in all of your credit reports explaining the circumstances.

FINANCIAL PLANNING *from* WE *to* ME

WORKSHEET 7A

JOINT LIABILITIES

	Liability/Debt Descriptions	Balance	Date & Source of Data	% Interest Rate	Post Separation Payments	Allocated to Husband or Wife
1						
2						
3						
4						
5						
6						
7						
8						
9						
10						

CHAPTER EIGHT
The Roof Over Your Head

Do you really want to keep the house? Many homemakers do. They fall in love with their home—they've invested hours of their time and labor in the shaping of their home environment. They want to keep it because it is familiar and a controllable element in an often out-of-control situation. If they have children, the stability of the home is even more important. Their attitude is understandable.

What is not so easily understood is that this asset—the familiar rooms and staircases—can be a real cash drain as well as an income tax trap for an unwary spouse. The person who keeps the home in the divorce settlement takes on the responsibility of maintaining it during ownership. This can mean big expenses if there is any degree of deferred maintenance to catch up on. He or she can also be responsible for 100% of the costs of sale and capital gains taxes when it is sold. These taxes can be considerable, especially if the house shelters tax deferred gains from one or more previous homes. Of course, the untaxed gain could be rolled over upon sale into another residence, but only by purchasing a home of equal or greater value than the adjusted sales price of the previous home within two years. A purchase of a house of a lesser value will mean paying taxes on the lesser of the gain on the old home or the difference between the price of the old and new home.

Avoiding A Nasty Tax Surprise

Start by looking for IRS Form 2119 on the tax return in the year you purchased your present home. This should give you the necessary information about the true cost basis of the residence. You cannot simply use the amount you paid for the home. That number may be meaningless. If you owned one or more homes previously and rolled gains from these homes into your present residence to defer taxes on those gains, the cost basis on your present home is less than your expense-adjusted purchase price.

If you don't plan to sell the family residence during the dissolution, this then just becomes information about that particular asset. If you do need or want to liquidate the family home, this information is critical, as the taxes due on the gain as well as the cost of sale of the residence become debits to the value of the asset. In other words, you don't want to accept an asset as part of the property settlement and then immediately find its true value is reduced due to unexpected taxes, real estate commissions, and assorted other sales costs.

Purchasing A Replacement Residence

If the house is not awarded to either spouse but sold immediately after the divorce and the proceeds split, each spouse is responsible for one half the taxes on the gain. The deferral of taxes is then made easier because each spouse need only purchase a replacement residence worth one half of the adjusted sales price of the marital residence. They have two years before or after the sale in order to continue to defer taxation on capital gains.

A problem can result in using this rule if one spouse has moved out and has been out of the house too long. That spouse can lose the ability to "roll" his or her share of the capital gain portion into a new home because the family home may no longer qualify as his or her principal residence. The IRS regulations are not well defined in this area. Currently there is legislation under consideration by Congress to allow divorced spouses to roll the gains from a marital residence as long as they lived there at least one day of the two year period. Check with a tax professional regarding the current status of this legislation.

The $125,000 Solution

Another tax benefit that is impacted by divorce is the $125,000 one time capital gains exclusion on a residence. Every economic unit (couple or single) is entitled to a $125,000 once in a lifetime exclusion of capital gains from tax. This benefit is available beginning at age 55, but generally to qualify one must have owned the subject home for the last five years and lived in it three out of the five years. If the residence is sold before the divorce and one spouse is eligible for and uses the exclusion, $125,000 of the profits would be protected from tax but the other spouse would lose eligibility to ever use this tax break. However, if the residence is sold *after* the divorce and both spouses are age 55 or older, each has the option to use their own exclusion or roll over the proceeds. Each party stands then on his or her own eligibility and can act independently of the other. This could allow an exemption of up to $250,000 gain on the sale of the home.

Following are a couple of examples of the tax impacts due to the timing of a house sale during a divorce situation.

A. Sam and Sally Smith, ages 40 and 45, own a $400,000 house. Sally cannot afford to keep the home after the divorce, so they put it up for sale shortly after Sam moves out.

Market Price of House:	$400,000
Costs of Sale =10% of Value:	<$ 40,000>
Adjusted Sales Price	$360,000

Sam and Sally each plan to purchase a new residence worth $180,000. Because the sale was part of the divorce, Sam shared in the costs to sell the house, and all of the capital gain from the sale was split evenly and rolled into their new respective residences. Result: no current taxation.

B. Jack and Janet Jones, ages 60 and 56, decide to split up. They sell their $300,000 house with a tax cost basis of $100,000. If they sold the house during the marriage, they would be able to exclude only $125,000 of the gain from taxes, leaving $75,000 subject to tax, and neither one would be able to use the exemption again. However, if they wait until after the divorce to sell the house, they could each use their own $125,000 exemption and shelter all of the taxable profits from taxation.

Alternatively, if Janet wanted to roll her share into a replacement residence, she could preserve her exemption while Jack used his for his share of the proceeds.

EXAMPLE 8A

RESIDENCE SALES TAX WORKSHEET

Sam & Sally Smith, Ages 40 & 45

		HUSBAND	WIFE
	Date Marital Residence Purchased		6/75
	Date of Sale of Marital Residence		7/95
	Value of Replacement Residence to be Purchased	$200,000	$200,000
1.	Selling price less expenses		$400,000
	Real estate commissions	$17,500	
	Loan fees	$0	
	All other associated closing costs	$8,000	
2.	Total selling costs. Include this number as a liability on the property allocation worksheet		$25,500
3.	Net amount realized (Line 1 less Line 2)		$374,500
4.	Basis of residence sold (take from tax return Form 2119 filed in year of residence purchase)		$150,000
	Closing costs not previously deducted	$0	
	Special assessments	$0	
	Land additions or sub-divisions	$0	
	Improvements to property (attach list)	$25,000	
	Less prior year's depreciation, energy credits, or casualty losses	$0	
	Adjusted basis		$175,000
5.	Gain or loss on sale (Line 1 minus Line 4). If no gain stop here. Taxes equal zero.		$199,500
6.	Divide the gain on the sale by two. This is the amount of gain to be assigned to each spouse.	99,750	$99,750

FINANCIAL PLANNING *from* WE *to* ME

		HUSBAND	WIFE
7.	Age 55 or over one time exclusion for each spouse. If house is sold after the divorce both spouses may be eligible. If not applicable, go to Line 7. Otherwise enter the smaller of line 5 or $125,000.	NA	NA
8.	Gain on sale (subtract Line 7 from Line 6). If zero, do not complete remainder of form. If more than zero and a new home was built or purchased by either spouse, go to Line 9. All others, stop. This is your taxable gain. Multiply your tax bracket or the top capital gains tax rate against this number and include as a tax liability on your property allocation worksheet.	$99,750	$99,750
9.	Fix-up expenses on old residence divided proportionately.	$0	$0
10.	Adjusted sales price of old residence (subtract line 7 and Line 9 from Line 3).	$187,250	$187,250
11.	Basis of new residence		
	Cost of new residence	$200,000	$200,000
	Closing costs	$2,000	$2,000
	Improvements to be made within 24 months of sale date.	$0	$0
11.	Total basis of new residence	$202,000	$202,000
12.	Subtract Line 11 from Line 10	($14,750)	($14,750)
13.	Taxable Gain on Sale (enter smaller of Line 8 or Line 12). Include these combined numbers as a liability on your Property Division	$0	$0
14.	Postponed gain (subtract Line 13 from Line 8).	$99,750	$99,750
15.	Adjusted basis of new home for each spouse. Subtract Line 14 from Line 11)	$102,250	$102,250

Chapter Eight—The Roof Over Your Head

WORKSHEET 8A

RESIDENCE SALES TAX CALCULATIONS

Date Marital Residence Purchased

Date of Sale of Marital Residence

	HUSBAND	WIFE

Value of Replacement Residence to be Purchased

1. Selling price less expenses

    Real estate commissions

    Loan fees

    All other associated closing costs

2. Total selling costs. Include this number as a liability on the property allocation worksheet

3. Net amount realized (Line 1 less Line 2)

4. Basis of residence sold (take from tax return Form 2119 filed in year of residence purchase)

    Closing costs not previously deducted

    Special assessments

    Land additions or sub-divisions

    Improvements to property (attach list)

    Less prior year's depreciation, energy credits, or casualty losses

    Adjusted basis

5. Gain or loss on sale (Line 1 minus Line 4). If no gain stop here. Taxes equal zero.

6. Divide the gain on the sale by two. This is the amount of gain to be assigned to each spouse.

FINANCIAL PLANNING *from* WE *to* ME

		HUSBAND	WIFE
7.	Age 55 or over one time exclusion for each spouse. If house is sold after the divorce both spouses may be eligible. If not applicable, go to Line 7. Otherwise enter the smaller of line 5 or $125,000.	_____	_____
8.	Gain on sale (subtract Line 7 from Line 6). If zero, do not complete remainder of form. If more than zero and a new home was built or purchased by either spouse, go to Line 9. All others, stop. This is your taxable gain. Multiply your tax bracket or the top capital gains tax rate against this number and include as a tax liability on your property allocation worksheet.	_____	_____
9.	Fix-up expenses on old residence divided proportionately.	_____	_____
10.	Adjusted sales price of old residence (subtract line 7 and Line 9 from Line 3).	_____	_____
11.	Basis of new residence	_____	_____
	Cost of new residence	_____	_____
	Closing costs	_____	_____
	Improvements to be made within 24 months of sale date.	_____	_____
11.	Total basis of new residence	_____	_____
12.	Subtract Line 11 from Line 10	_____	_____
13.	Taxable Gain on Sale (enter smaller of Line 8 or Line 12). Include these combined numbers as a liability on your Property Division	_____	_____
14.	Postponed gain (subtract Line 13 from Line 8).	_____	_____
15.	Adjusted basis of new home for each spouse. Subtract Line 14 from Line 11)	_____	_____

CHAPTER NINE
Dividing The Retirement Nest Egg Without Breaking The Yolk

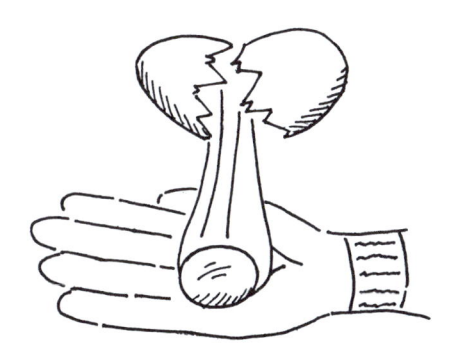

IRAs, 403(b) plans (TSAs), Keogh plans, and company defined contribution plans such as ESOPs and 401(k) plans are generally divisible in a divorce and as such can be transferred from one spouse's account to the other's. Because these plans are usually tax deferred, giving one spouse the lion's share will cause a tax burden down the road when the money is withdrawn.

It's Your Money Too

A QDRO or Qualified Domestic Relations Order allows transfer of qualified tax-deferred assets from one spouse to another and is drawn up by your attorney. The funds must go from the plan directly to the receiving spouse (alternate payee) or the receiving spouse's IRA. If the money is sent directly to the alternate payee it will trigger an automatic 20% tax withholding. If the alternate payee had intended to deposit all the money in his or her IRA, it could now be difficult. As an example, if $150,000 were distributed to you, $30,000 would be withheld by the IRS. By default, you could end up paying tax on dollars you intended to put in your IRA if you could not replace the withheld $30,000. The IRS won't help—they will keep the 20% of withheld taxes until the following year when you file your income tax return. All this can be avoided by having the plan trustee transfer the money directly into your own IRA.

The only good news in this story is that a 10% penalty tax will not apply. The law excludes QDRO transferred money from the 10% under 59-1/2 penalty. The alternate payee could then elect within 60 days to make a full, if possible, or partial deposit to his or her IRA to continue to defer the taxes on that portion. Or, he or she can pay the federal income tax and have free access to the money.

Once the money is deposited into an IRA, the 10% tax penalty again applies to any future withdrawals before age 59-1/2 except under certain narrow exceptions.

Nailing Down The Values

Be sure that your decree states a minimum amount to be transferred or your percent share of the balance at separation (whichever is higher) via the QDRO. Don't forget to include a pro rata share of any increase in value due to appreciation since date of separation. Typically the QDRO is the last piece of paperwork to be completed in the dissolution process except for your attorney's last billing. Delays due to technical glitches could be a problem if the investment is fluctuating in value.

Change Of IRA Ownership

Dividing an IRA is a simpler matter. Generally, the most efficient method is to leave each person with his or her respective IRAs. If an IRA must be transferred to balance the asset division, it is done by decree rather than by the QDRO used to transfer pension, profit sharing, 403(b), 401(k) or other qualified retirement programs.

SEPP Your IRA

Yes, you can avoid paying tax on a large retirement plan distribution and still create cashflow—even if you are under 59-1/2. No one wants to recognize federal income tax on a large IRA lump sum years before it is necessary. It only makes sense to earn interest on the government's tax dollar as long as possible. The challenge is for the under 59-1/2 year old to make IRA withdrawals without incurring the 10% excise tax penalty. This is allowed under a provision called the 72(t) exception. If one takes annual distributions based on life expectancy and a reasonable interest rate and continues those distributions each and every year at the same rate until they are age 59-1/2 and for a minimum of five years, it works.

The following chart gives you a factor to multiple times each $100 in your IRA accounts to estimate your penalty free annual withdrawal. Choose the age you will become in the year you are contemplating a withdrawal. This is the amount that must be taken as a SEPP (Systematic Early Periodic Payments) if you wish to avoid the 10% penalty.

FACTORS BASED ON A 7.5% INTEREST RATE ASSUMPTION

Age	Factor	Age	Factor
40	7.7776	50	8.1496
41	7.8040	51	8.2134
42	7.8399	52	8.2820
43	7.8708	53	8.3557
44	7.9113	54	8.3763
45	7.9476	55	8.4611
46	7.9936	56	8.5529
47	8.0426	57	8.6523
48	8.0889	58	8.7604
49	8.0901	59	8.8128

You can be any age and start this system. We have elected to only illustrate factors for those 40 and older. The earlier this system is started, the more years of regulated withdrawals are required.

Caution—once you start this SEPP withdrawal program, you cannot take any extra withdrawals from that IRA. If you do, you will destroy the SEPP plan. Not only will those extra dollars be subject to the 10% tax penalty, but the tax penalty will also be retroactively applied to all distributions in previous tax years. The only winner in this situation would be the IRS.

Dividing A Future Pension Annuity

Vested pension benefits in defined benefit pension plans earned during the marriage are generally considered to be marital property.

Note that in a long term marriage there may be pensions from more than one employer if a spouse worked for more than five years with different companies. This includes military pensions and state and federal civil service pensions. Check with

Chapter Nine—Dividing The Retirement Nest Egg

each employer for the years of service required for vesting. Valuing these benefits is complex and often requires the services of an accountant or other financial professional who is experienced with present value calculations.

In order to value these benefits, contact the employer for a statement of current vested pension benefits. You will ideally want the amount of vested pension benefits you or your spouse would receive if employment were terminated immediately or at the date of legal separation based on the earliest possible retirement age. Keep in mind that only the portion earned during the marriage is marital property. Any credit for future years of service or for years of service prior to the marriage will be the separate property of the spouse who earned it. Because the value of a pension is directly related to the number of years payments may be received (life expectancy of the retiree), special allowances may need to be made for persons with serious health problems. If this applies in your situation, discuss this with your attorney.

Present Value Of Future Pension

A pension can be split one of two ways: The first option is to give all of the present value of the vested pension benefits to the spouse who earned it. The other spouse would receive offsetting assets in exchange. This may be the only option with some pension plans, particularly some union plans, which may not have any mechanism to pay out benefits to a member's ex-spouse. See the information in the Resource Section for further clarification. This method has a big benefit—tax advantage. Generally speaking, you can trade a fully taxable pension share for another asset where the deferred tax is nil or less than the pension. Just don't trade away valuable income producing assets like a pension for depreciating use assets such as over-inflated valuations for furnishings or luxury automobiles. On page 76, you will find an example of a present value of a pension.

Years Of Marriage/Years Of Service Formula

The second option is only available for those pension plans that have the ability to split the actual pension benefit payments between the two spouses, effectively giving each person a smaller pension. This technique is most applicable in long term marriages where the parties are close to or already retired.

The most equitable way to divide a future pension benefit, some of which was earned during the marriage and some which would be earned after the divorce, is to apply the following formula:

$$\text{Pension Amount} \times \frac{\text{Years of Marriage}}{\text{Years of Service}} \times \text{Agreed Upon \% Split}$$

This formula calculates the pension amount to be awarded to the non-employee spouse. The remaining pension benefit remains with the employee spouse. The primary reason to use this formula is fairness. Many pensions have calculation formulas which use a percentage of pay times salary times years of service. It seems only fair that the spouse who endured through the vesting and years growing toward that final calculation should share in it based on the time spent in the marriage. Consider the following pension result using a straight division of the current vested benefit versus the Years of Marriage/Years of Service formula.

Sam & Sally Smith, married 20 years, years of service 20 years

    Sam's current vested pension benefit $2,000/Mo
    50% awarded to Sally $1,000/Mo

Sam & Sally Smith, married 20 years, years of service 30 years.

Chapter Nine—Dividing The Retirement Nest Egg

Sam's expected future pension $4,000/Mo

Future expected pension if husband works additional 10 years.

Yrs. of Marriage/Yrs. of Service share to Sally $1,340/Mo

$$\$4,000 \times \frac{20}{30} = \$2,640 \times 50\% = \$1,340$$

Future Pension Issues

Another possible reason to take a piece of a future pension annuity payment rather than be bought out at the time of the divorce is that some pension plans allow retirees to receive a subsidized medical or Medicare supplement health insurance plan. By receiving a separate pension, the non-employee spouse may retain eligibility for potentially valuable insurance benefits. For example, the divorced spouse of a career military person can qualify for subsidized medical coverage if he or she was married to that person during a full 20 years of military service. If the marriage and service overlap is even one day short of 20 years, the non-military spouse loses these privileges. Check with your pension department to see if options such as this are available in your or your spouse's plan.

Beware! A disadvantage to this method is that sometimes the non-employee spouse must wait until the employee is old enough to retire or actually does retire before he or she can tap his or her portion of the pension. This can apply even if the divided pension has been set aside in a separate account for the alternate payee spouse.

This can be a major problem if the employee is much younger than the ex-spouse. If the pension is not officially divided until retirement, the spouse could lose his or her share of the pension upon the employee's demise. Another major risk to the non-employee spouse is that many pension plans cannot guarantee post-retirement survival benefits to him or her if the employee spouse dies. In both these cases, it is important that the non-employee spouse obtain life insurance coverage on his or her ex-spouse to cover the potential loss of benefits.

EXAMPLE 9A

MILITARY PENSION PLAN PRESENT VALUE CALCULATION

Date of Birth	7/1/50
Current Age	45
Date of Marriage	9/30/75
Date of Separation	1/1/95
Years of Military Service	7/68-6/88
Years of Credited Service at Separation	20
Years of Credited Service During Marriage	12.75
Percent of Pension Earned During Marriage	74.62
Age at Earliest Eligible Retirement Date	Now Retired
Life Expectancy Based on Current Age	74.62[1]
Annual Pension Benefit Collectable Now (taken from Department of Defense Retiree Account Statement giving the current rate of pay. Pension amount used is taxable portion of gross pension after deductions for VA waiver and survivor benefit costs).	$20,556
Annual cost of living adjustment assumption based on the CPI index for all urban wage earners and clerical workers.	3%

Chapter Nine—Dividing The Retirement Nest Egg

ANNUAL PENSION ESTIMATES THROUGH LIFE EXPECTANCY

AGE	YEAR	$ AMOUNT	AGE	YEAR	$ AMOUNT
45	1995	20,556.00	61	2011	32,986.00
46	1996	21,572.68	62	2012	33,975.94
47	1997	21,807.86	63	2013	34,995.21
48	1998	22,462.10	64	2014	36,045.07
49	1999	23,135.96	65	2015	37,126.42
50	2000	23,830.04	66	2016	38,240.22
51	2001	24,544.94	67	2017	39,387.42
52	2002	25,281.29	68	2018	40,569.04
53	2003	26,039.73	69	2019	41,786.12
54	2004	26,820.92	70	2020	43,039.70
55	2005	27,625.55	71	2021	44,330.89
56	2006	28,454.31	72	2022	45,660.82
57	2007	29,307.94	73	2023	47,030.64
58	2008	30,187.18	74	2024	48,441.56
59	2009	31,092.79	75	2025	30,934.78[2]
60	2010	32,025.58			

Discount Interest Rate[3]	7%
Current Present Value	$353,835
Marital Portion of Pension Current Present Value	$225,570

1. Life expectancy based on 1980 Washington State Commissioner's standard mortality table.
2. Reflects partial year.
3. Annual discount used.

CHAPTER TEN
Pathways To The Future

If you're anywhere under 55, reasonably healthy and not in the workplace, get ready. You will probably be faced with making decisions about how you will earn your keep. In many traditional marriages it is common for one spouse, usually the wife, to place her career on hold in order to better manage the household and care for the couple's children. This works out just swell if the marriage continues happily ever after. But what about the 50% of not-so-happily-ever-after marriages that end in divorce?

If it was a long term marriage, get ready to join the ranks of displaced homemakers.

Career Resuscitation

When the displaced homemaker tries to return to work after an extended hiatus, he or she often finds that job-related skills are rusty and may be out of touch with technological changes that have impacted many industries. As a returning worker he or she may need to take classes or renew licenses before becoming fully employable. A good paying job that was available 10 or 20 years ago may have been altered dramatically today by technology or perhaps eliminated entirely. What if you have never worked? In these cases, re-education or new education is clearly mandated.

A decision made on behalf of the family for one spouse to stay at home leads to that spouse's economic deprivation at time of divorce. For the most part this is an issue which impacts more women than men. I have, though, dealt with men in this situation. I once testified in the case of a professional man who, due to his wife's separate property, became a househusband. Her net worth allowed the couple to lead a life of leisure. After 20 years the husband had lost his professional expertise as well as his desire to be employed in his former field. As a result, he was awarded a portion of his wife's separate (non-marital) property to compensate him for the loss of his career skills.

The High Cost Of Not Working

The biggest impact of a long term hiatus from a career is the loss in seniority and resulting lower re-entry wage base. Often the returning worker has to start at or near the bottom of the pay ladder. One way to illustrate the opportunity cost to the stay-at-home spouse or the spouse who had to give up career

Chapter Ten—Pathways To The Future

opportunities in order to follow a higher earning spouse to greener pastures is to present an opportunity cost table. On page 84 you will find examples of one approach. This approach simply takes the current earnings gap and discounts it over some specified period of time.

Lost years of service directly impact that spouse's ability to accumulate retirement benefits and will also result in lower Social Security benefits based on that person's personal earnings record. Many pension plan programs are calculated using some form of average final pay and years of service. In addition, eligibility for early retirement at unreduced benefits is also often predicated on years of service. A person with 30 years of service may be able to retire at 55 or 60, while someone with only 10 years may need to work until age 65.

My Story

I know all about this as I was the homemaker mother who worked sporadically, alternating working years with child bearing and mothering. In addition, my last child had a speech disability which required me to taxi him to special schools, plus my husband wouldn't "let me work." Upon my divorce, I had to find a job fast. With rusty skills, I struck out as best I could but soon found that I needed education to be employable at a "living" wage.

So at the tender age of 39, single mother of three, Kathleen Cotton became a college student while working full time. Yes, it worked out—I did get a degree and went on to build over the course of many years a viable new career, but it was not easy. No social life, no leisure time, no steady paycheck, no vacation pay, no retirement plan, no discretionary dollars and no end in sight. It wasn't until about 10 years after our divorce that I was able to start burying my "bag lady" fears.

During that same time period, my ex-husband was getting promoted, at the peak of his career, saving excess dollars into retirement plans, becoming fully vested, and enjoying an abundance of leisure time.

The $64,000 Question

My story is not unlike that of many, many women and a few men. Their reality is being asked to make a decision on what type of work they want to pursue at the conclusion of the divorce. For many, this is like being asked what they want to "be" when they grow up. They don't know because they have not given this a thought during the years they stayed home to raise children or make a comfortable home for a more career-oriented spouse. The only way they can even begin to grasp the parameters of such a decision is to consult with a career counselor who, after a battery of tests, may be able to help steer the displaced homemaker to a field in which he or she has the talent to develop the requisite skills.

Career Counselors Can Put Life In Your Workday

Career counselors are frequently retained by dissolution attorneys early on in the process when it involves a long term marriage/homemaker spouse. These counselors help the individuals determine what type of training is required to enter or advance in a given field. This is a very difficult issue. Imagine trying to decide in the course of just a few short months—the time between your separation and your actual divorce—just exactly what you want to do for the next 5-10-20 years. It's mind boggling, but it can also be a great opportunity to get it right. Yes, you can love to work if you find the right niche for your abilities and talents. Take the time to work with a career counselor who can guide you to the appropriate career field. It will soon become apparent whether or not you need to go back

Chapter Ten—Pathways To The Future

to school. If you do, you won't be alone. Colleges and universities are full of middle-aged women and a few men who are getting degrees due to broken marriages. It is not uncommon for these older students to be funded in this effort by spousal support.

FINANCIAL PLANNING *from* WE *to* ME

EXAMPLE 10A

QUANTIFICATION OF CAREER OPPORTUNITY COST TO MARITAL COMMUNITY AND DISCOUNTED WAGE POTENTIAL DUE TO CHILD CARE/HOMEMAKER COMMITMENT

Year	Sally Smith Occupation	Actual Wages[1]	Estimated Possible Wages[2]	Total Foregone Wages
1975	Registered Nurse	$23,722	$23,722	$0
1976	Same	24,434	24,434	0
1977	Same	25,167	25,167	0
1978	Same	25,922	25,922	0
1979	1st child born in August	13,350	26,699	13,350
1980	Child care/homemaker	0	27,500	27,500
1981	2nd child born - Child care/homemaker	0	28,325	28,325
1982	Same	0	29,175	29,175
1983	Same	0	30,050	30,050
1984	3rd child born	0	30,952	30,952
1985	Child care/homemaker	0	31,880	31,880
1986	Same	0	32,827	32,837
1987	Same	0	33,822	33,822
1988	Same	0	34,837	34,837
1989	Same	0	35,882	35,882
1990	Same	0	36,958	36,958
1991	Return to work 1/2 time as RN	14,279	38,067	23,788
1992	Same	14,707	39,209	24,501
1993	Same	15,149	40,385	25,237
1994	Work full time as RN	31,206	41,597	41,597
	Total foregone earnings during marriage			$449,484

1. Actual historical earnings as provided by Sally Smith
2. Potential income from 1974 through 1994 based on information provided by career counselor after discussion with Sally Smith and review of her education and work experience in each year. Full time salary assumed to increase at 3% per year.

EXAMPLE 10B

FUTURE EARNINGS PROJECTION COMPARED WITH POTENTIAL OPPORTUNITY COST DUE TO LACK OF WORK EXPERIENCE

Year	Sally Smith Occupation	Actual Wages[1]	Estimated Potential Wages[2]	Opportunity Cost
1995	Work full time as RN/Child care	$32,142	$42,845	$10,702
1996	Same	32,142	42,845	10,702
1997	Same	32,142	42,845	10,702
1998	Same	32,142	42,845	10,702
1999	Same	32,142	42,845	10,702
2000	Same	32,142	42,845	10,702
2001	Same	32.142	42,845	10,702
2002	Work full time, youngest is 18	32,142	42,845	10,702
2003	Work full time as RN	32,142	42,845	10,702
2004	Same	32.142	42,845	10,702
2005	Same	32,142	42,845	10,702
2006	Same	32,142	42,845	10,702
2007	Same	32,142	42,845	10,702
2008	Same	32,142	42,845	10,702
2009	Same	32,142	42,845	10,702
2010	Same	32,142	42,845	10,702
2011	Same	32,142	42,845	10,702
2012	Same	32,142	42,845	10,702
2013	Same	32,142	42,845	10,702
2014	Same	32,142	42,845	10,702
2015	Same	32,142	42,845	10,702
	Present value of opportunity cost due to loss of career experience during marriage. Future loss of earning ability discounted to present at 7%.			$121,313

1. Projected future expected and potential salaries not shown increasing in the future.
2. Projected future full time salary if Sally Smith had been continuously employed during the marriage.

CHAPTER ELEVEN
Whose Balloon's Bigger

Social Security is the one asset where value is often ignored in the process of dissolving marriages. As an income stream attached to the worker who earned it, it is not a divisible asset. Yet it must not be overlooked as an asset of value that frequently benefits one spouse more than the other. As shown in the drawing, one person's Social Security balloon could be twice as large or more, depending on the length of the marriage.

Crumbs From Social Security

Spouses who have done minimal work outside of the home and either have very little or no Social Security benefits of their own must rely on their spouse's earning record for their benefit calculation. This situation has probably occurred due to a joint decision by both spouses that one would be the homemaker or perhaps just the "cake earner" (fun money) spouse. This arrangement can work fine if the parties stay married but will penalize the lower earner if divorce occurs.

Another example where this occurs is when one spouse was an unpaid and unofficial employee of a family business. This is frequently the case when by paying all of the family business earnings to one person, that person can exceed the Social Security tax income limit and reduce the family's total tax burden. The other spouse works but does not get paid, i.e., no payroll taxes due. That spouse when divorced walks away with a minimal, if any, earnings record of his/her own.

Collecting On Your EX

GOOD NEWS! A divorced spouse can collect Social Security benefits based on his or her former spouse's earning record if he or she 1) was married to them for 10 or more years; 2) has been divorced for two years; 3) is at least age 62; and 4) has not remarried. Remarriage will cause a person to lose all spousal Social Security benefit eligibility from a prior marriage. But if that subsequent marriage should fail, the individual is again eligible to draw against whichever spouse he or she was married to for more than 10 years. Note that the spousal benefit can only be drawn when the petitioner is age 62, or age 60 if the widow of an ex-spouse. The person the benefit is being drawn against does not have to be on Social Security but does have to be at least age 62 or deceased.

BAD NEWS! The benefit is only equal to half of the worker's benefit. The worker will still collect 100% of his or her benefit. The government allocates a benefit to the qualifying ex-spouse of up to 50% of the worker's age 65 benefit. For example, if the ex-spouse draws at age 62, the benefit is 37.5% of the age 65 benefit. If the ex-spouse waits until age 65, it is the full 50%. If you are an ex-spouse widow or widower, the benefit is 71.5% of the worker's benefit if you start collecting benefits at age 60, 80% if you start at age 62, and 100% if you wait until age 65 to draw. My mother recently found this out as she applied to collect her Social Security benefits on my stepfather. She discovered that the Social Security benefits available from her 25 year marriage to my father were greater than those she could collect based on her second husband's earning history.

It's Not Fair

Here is an example of how disparate Social Security benefits can add up. The full impact of this economic disparity can be seen by discounting the future Social Security income benefits from John who will draw $1,000 per month during his retirement and Susan who will draw $500/month against John's benefit. For purposes of this analysis, both benefits have been increased by a 3% yearly cost of living adjustment up to each spouse's age 85. We have also made the assumption they are both 65 and eligible for their full benefit. In order to bring the yearly income stream payable to life expectancy or beyond back to today's present value, we have discounted this benefit by an assumed interest rate of 7%.

Susan's Present Value Benefit	John's Present Value Benefit
$82,607	$165,214

The result speaks for itself. The only way to fully rectify this imbalance is to shift compensating assets to the spouse with the lower Social Security benefit. The best way to illustrate this disparity is a simple present value analysis as shown above or with a long term analysis depicting net worth disparity.

CHAPTER TWELVE
Over My Dead Body

"I'M SORRY IT SAYS HERE YOU FORGOT TO CHANGE YOUR BENEFICIARIES"

Thinking about who will get what should you die is a good exercise to do now. It concerns updating the beneficiary designations on all life insurance policies, IRAs, annuities, and retirement programs. Also review and update your will and any living trust arrangements that you have set up.

Will You Or Won't You

Do this as soon as it appears that your marriage is irrevocably broken. Don't wait until after the divorce. Consider the effects of your demise during the divorce on the distribution of your portion of the marital assets. Do you want your soon-to-be ex-spouse to receive your share of the estate or life insurance proceeds? The answer is usually, "Hardly!" Unless you change your will your spouse will share in your estate until a separate property agreement is signed or a decree of divorce is entered.

In some circumstances, you may be forced to leave an ex-spouse as a beneficiary on a life insurance policy. If you are paying child support and/or maintenance, you may be required to name the recipient as the beneficiary of your life insurance policy until the support obligation is complete.

Own A Piece Of Their Rock

The preferred way to protect an income stream such as child support or spousal maintenance is for the payee to own life insurance on the payer in an amount sufficient to replace any lost payments should the payer die. Additionally, the payee must be the beneficiary. If there is not an existing policy, it is advisable for the support recipient to obtain a policy insuring the support payer. Most spouses would not have an objection to serving as the insured "body" for this purpose. The life insurance provides a measure of security to the payee that he or she would not lose the child support and/or spousal maintenance if the payer were to die. The insurance policy should be specifically identified in the divorce decree to avoid any possible contention over the right of the ex-spouse to receive insurance benefits.

Life Insurance Premiums As Alimony

Life insurance premiums can be added to the base spousal support paid by the support provider to the payee. The advantage to this is a full tax deduction of the amount paid. In order to qualify a segregated insurance premium payment as alimony, it must be required by decree, and payment must end upon the beneficiary's death. The payee needs to be the owner of the insurance policy, with his or her economic interest in the policies subject to no contingencies. In order for this to work on an existing life insurance policy, the ownership would have to be transferred to the ex-spouse/beneficiary.

Negotiate For Life

Don't forget to consider this important step. If you are to receive an income stream of any kind from your ex-spouse, ask your attorney to include life insurance coverage in the negotiation package so that it can be included as a fixed provision in the decree.

CHAPTER THIRTEEN
A COBRA You Can Love

One of your major considerations if you have not been employed will be what to do about health insurance. You may need to buy a new policy or you may be able to continue for a while under an existing policy carried through your spouse's place of employment. As mentioned earlier in Chapter One, the Congressional Omnibus Budget Reconciliation Act of 1986 (COBRA) is available to you for up to 36 months if your spouse was covered under a group plan and worked for a company with more than 20 employees. Remember that this cost comes out of your pocket, not the employer's, and is only a temporary solution at best. There is a very short period of time, generally

30 days or less, to apply for COBRA benefits after the divorce is final.

Comparing Policies

Eligibility to continue existing health insurance is an excellent benefit to a spouse with poor health or pre-existing conditions. If you are in good health, however, you should check policy benefits and premium costs at several different insurers as you may want to switch to a less expensive or different type of coverage.

Health care regulations are in a state of flux as states scramble to adapt to new Federal laws. In Washington State, for instance, all health insurance companies must issue policies to all applicants regardless of health, and can only exclude health conditions from coverage for a maximum period of three months which are found in a three month look-back at your medical history. This is a priceless benefit for anyone with poor health or pre-existing conditions as they are guaranteed to be able to obtain coverage without paying extra "special risk" premiums. If you need the COBRA coverage you will generally pay for it unless your spouse is ordered by the court or agrees in writing (in the decree) to cover this expense for you.

Self-Insured Plans

Companies such as Boeing which utilize self-insured health plans are not currently included under this new state law but are covered under federal COBRA requirements. Call your spouse's employee benefits office for information on his or her specific plan.

Insuring The Children

Children can be covered under either parent's plan regardless of who has custody. Generally, if one spouse has a employer-provided benefit which provides for family coverage at a subsidized price, it is most appropriate to keep the children on that policy. Your divorce papers should state specifically who is to provide and pay for the children's medical and dental insurance premiums. Child support can be adjusted for out-of-pocket health insurance costs for the children which fall disproportionately on one parent.

CHAPTER FOURTEEN
Your Fair Share Campaign

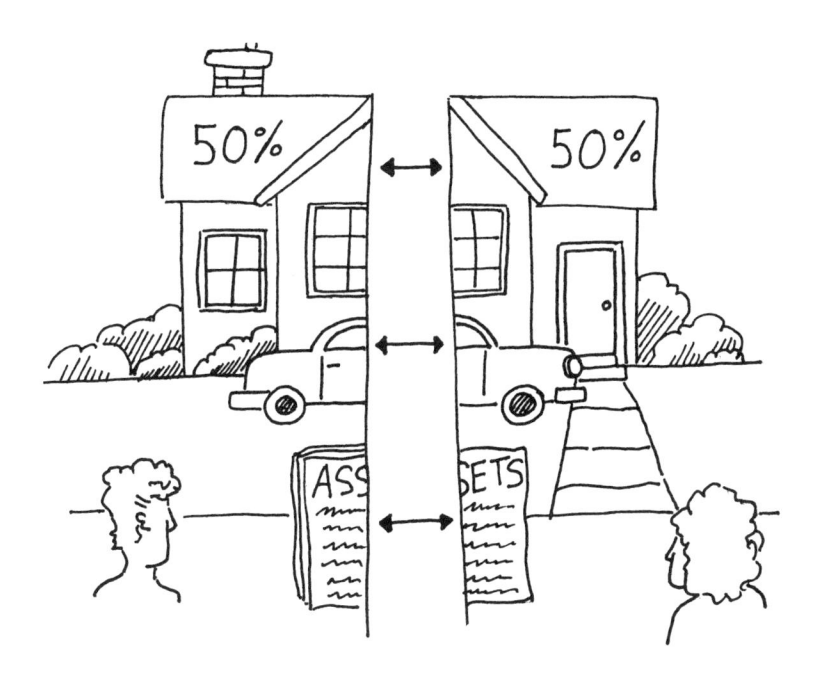

This chapter deals with a difficult reality—50/50 may not be fair. A major goal in the dissolution process is to achieve some level of economic parity, i.e., financial equality, between the spouses for an appropriate period after the divorce. However, it is a rare marriage where both partners have equal education, job experience, and earning potential. These differences often result in long term financial disparity between the spouses and are a cause for concern in the break-up of long term marriages. Tangible financial disparity can occur in areas such as potential earning power, job benefits, and/or lost career opportunities. Intangible but still important disparity can exist in who "owned" the financial savvy during the marriage.

Use It Or Lose It

Lose what? Your earning power. It happens all the time. One spouse worked at a job for pay and the other worked at home for no pay. Both contributed value to the marriage. The big difference is in how they were rewarded. Tangible reward is the name of this game. Money, seniority, and experience belong to the spouse who brought in the dollars. The other spouse may not have a job, let alone experience, training, or education. Or, if that spouse did work at one time, he or she may be woefully out-of-date in his or her field. This obviously varies from marriage to marriage. Both spouses may have worked from the beginning of their marriage yet one may have traded off career opportunities for quality of life issues. One can say he or she made that choice, but usually these choices evolve from partnership type decisions on what kind of marital lifestyle is desired by both parties.

Vacations, Sick Pay And Other Niceties Of Life

Employee benefits are worth bucks. These range from eligibility for health, disability and life insurance at greatly subsidized costs, to vacation, sick pay, bonuses, retirement pensions, and pre-tax retirement investment plans with matching company contributions. Again, one spouse may be basking in these benefits and the other may be faced with working for hourly wages with no benefits.

Financial Savvy

Yes, this is worth money too. Subtle, yet distinct differences in the ability to prosper depends on who has financial knowledge of the marital assets and liabilities. One party may have "owned" it during the marriage, which leaves the other party in financial kindergarten and easy prey for poor financial advice. I recently encountered a client in this situation. Her husband did all of the investing during the marriage. When they divorced, he gave her a list of investments to consider for her $300,000 share of the retirement benefits. The problem was that she lacked knowledge about this area. How could she make a good decision? As a result, she was forced to hire a money manager to help her manage her investments. He was not.

Career Costs

In terms of ability to earn a decent wage, this issue usually applies to women who have been married for 15 or more years to a man who has been the major income producer of the family unit. These women may have interrupted their education or career or never even got started for many possible reasons: husband's job promotions that took the family to different geographic locales, or the couple decided that the wife would be a part-time or full-time homemaker/mother. The net effect is the same—lower earning potential for the non-working spouse.

It is difficult for the higher wage earner to conceptualize the gross disparity in lifestyle that can occur due to income disparity. Most individuals feel they are "getting taken to the cleaners" when they are requested to give the lower earning spouse more than 50% of the property and perhaps even some spousal support. But listen to what judges and attorneys in the state of Washington have said about this issue:

"In the case of a long marriage, the goal should be to look

forward and seek to place the spouses in an economic position where, if they both work to the reasonable limits of their respective earning capacities and manage the properties awarded to them reasonably, they can be expected to be in roughly equal financial positions for the rest of their lives. Long term maintenance, sometimes permanent, is presumably likely to be used unless the properties accumulated are quite substantial, so that a lopsided award of property would permit a balancing of the positions without maintenance." Judge Robert Winsor, **Guidelines for the Exercise of Judicial Discretion in Marriage Dissolutions**, 14 Washington State Bar News 114-19 (January 1982).

"Women feel aggrieved in property division during divorce. They claim their husbands often have superior knowledge of family finances and may be in a position to hide assets. Wives also fault the courts for failure to recognize the opportunity cost of homemaking and how long the difference in economic circumstances between the parties will prevail after the divorce. Women often end up being forced to sell the property they receive." **Gender and Justice in the Courts**, Task Force Report (August 1989).

What, then, can the courts do with women or men caught in this dilemma? They can allocate extra dollars from settlements for education plus spousal support to assist them during a retraining period, for starters. Regardless of how much help is given to the non-working or economically disadvantaged spouse, he or she may never catch up financially to the spouse who is fully established in a career. The only way to alleviate part of this disparity is through disparate settlements and the sharing through spousal maintenance of jointly built career assets.

Work May Not Be In The Cards

If the marriage has been very long and the non-worker spouse is in his or her late 50s, he or she may not be expected to

Chapter Fourteen—Your Fair Share Campaign

go to work at all. After all, his or her life was planned and those plans may not have included the expectation of working outside the home. In addition, the benefits of training and education decrease dramatically when the homemaker spouse has only a few working years left to take advantage of any increased income. Health issues also come into play more commonly when the spouses are nearing retirement and can limit the future earnings ability of either the husband or the wife.

While we have used in this chapter references to men as well as women, the majority of the time these issues most often adversely affect the wife. What is the equitable solution? Consider the following:

Long Term Marriage

John and Susan, both age 55 and married for 30 years, are divorcing. John's attorney has proposed to Susan the following asset division:

Assets	Net Assets	John	Susan
House	$150,000		$150,000
Retirement Plan	350,000	250,000	100,000
Misc. Accounts	50,000	25,000	25,000
Life Ins. Cash	10,000		10,000
IRA #1	17,000	17,000	
IRA #2	11,000		11,000
Series EE	5,000		5,000
Household Goods	12,000	2,000	10,000
John's Car	20,000	20,000	
Susan's Car	5,000		5,000
		$314,000	$316,000

John makes $75,000 annually and plans to work until he is 65. He has access to a pension paid for by his employer and can contribute 12% to the company 401(k) plan. His employer contributes another 4%. Susan has only worked in clerical positions and this just during the past 10 years when their last child graduated from high school. She makes $18,000 annually working for a non-profit organization. Her firm does not have a pension plan, but they do have a retirement savings program. She has never contributed because John's plan was so good.

We do not even have to perform financial calculations to know that John and Susan face far different financial realities with this settlement offer than may be apparent on the surface. However, unless we run the numbers we'll never know just how disparate their futures will be.

To start with, we'll make an assumption that they should both be entitled to have comparable lifestyles for the rest of their lives based upon the length of time they have spent building a life together. Now, let's run those numbers and see what happens if Susan settles for the initial settlement volley. The result is definitely not what could be deemed fair or equitable.

The 50/50 Result

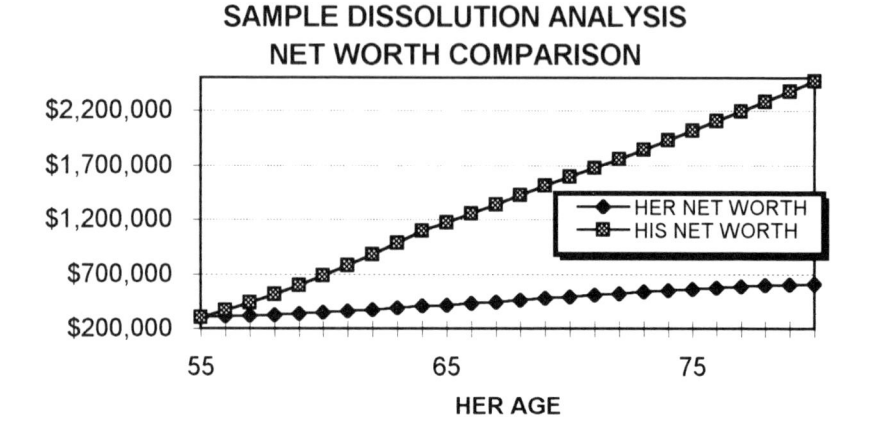

**SAMPLE DISSOLUTION ANALYSIS
NET WORTH COMPARISON**

HER NET WORTH
HIS NET WORTH

HER AGE

Reality Check

We couldn't close this chapter without cautioning that not all divorce solutions finish with the sought-after result. But the type of financial analysis we have discussed throughout this book can help close the disparity gap. When enough judges and attorneys understand that life-impacting decisions cannot be made based on settlement proposals that haven't evaluated where both parties will be in five, ten, or fifteen years, we will have started to level the playing field between high earner spouses and their domestic partners.

WORKSHEET 14A
PERSONAL DOCUMENTS REQUIRED FOR LONG TERM ANALYSIS

	Item or Statement Information	Required	Received	Not Applicable
1	Current paystubs for both spouses for three consecutive months.			
2	Copies of tax returns for previous three years - include all schedules.			
3	Information on regular bonuses received.			
4	Full income and expense information on any farms or businesses run by either spouse.			
5	Current income amounts and recent cost of living adjustments, if applicable, for any pension benefit currently being received.			
6	Projections of future earnings changes if additional education or career changes are anticipated.			
7	Calculated child support amounts.			
8	Temporary spousal support/alimony amounts and date of inception. Note any variation in amount paid.			
9	Pension plans - include following information: Projected benefit at planned retirement date, current vested benefit, any COLA adjustment to post-retirement benefits, the employee plan information book.			
10	Social Security projected benefits - if unavailable, a standard table will be used.			
11	Normal living expenses not including rent or mortgage payments.			

Chapter Fourteen—Your Fair Share Campaign

	Item or Statement Information	Required	Received	Not Applicable
12	Mortgages - Include the following: Interest rate, monthly principal and interest payment, current balance, years remaining.			
13	Rent - Monthly amount if applicable.			
14	Other expenses - Include all that apply: Counseling expenses, college costs for client, college costs for child(ren), number of quarters or semesters to attend, number of credits per quarter or semester, projected start and ending dates of applicable expenses.			
15	Statement copies and descriptions of all stocks, bonds, mutual funds, certificates of deposit, bank accounts, etc. Include purchase price if known. Include current and date of separation statements.			
16	Statement copies and descriptions of all IRAs, 401(k) plans, 403(b) plans, ESOP plans, profit sharing, etc. Include information on contribution amounts and any employer matching contributions (%). Also include beneficiary designations on all employer-sponsored programs. Include current and date of separation values.			
17	Statement copies and descriptions of any deferred compensation plans or arrangements (funded or unfunded). Include details on plan restrictions and current and date of separation values.			

FINANCIAL PLANNING *from* WE *to* ME

	Item or Statement Information	Required	Received	Not Applicable
18	Current cash values and death benefits of life insurance policies. Identify the owner, insured, and beneficiary.			
19	Installment sales contracts - include current balance, interest rate, and payment. Provide copy of original contract if available.			
20	Current appraisals on all real estate owned. Include cost basis in the property.			
21	Information on any loans or mortgages against real estate assets. Include the current balance, interest rate, and principal and interest payment amounts for each loan.			
22	Appraised value of any business owned. If the business is substantial, it must be evaluated by a business valuation specialist.			
23	Information and values of assets owned by or held in trust for minor children.			
24	A copy of any pre-marital agreements			
25	Copies of all credit card and personal loan statements. Include current and date of separation balances, interest rate, and minimum monthly payments. Note if any of these debts are secured by a particular asset.			
26	Appraisals of personal property, jewelry, collections, antiques, automobiles, etc.			

CHAPTER FIFTEEN
How Am I Going To Get Through This Mess?

Settling a divorce is not an easy task. One of the first steps should be to list your priorities in terms of the children (if any), your lifestyle, and your assets, as well as what you think your spouse's priorities will be. Do this before you start negotiating for property or support.

Can You Settle?

We have seen a few people settle their own divorce simply because they knew which button to push the hardest and in the process saved considerable legal fees. But, normally this doesn't work. Emotions run too hot and psyches can be too fragile to expose to confrontational warfare. To help you prioritize the issues, get out paper and pencil and copy down the following statements.

- My main concern for the children is:
- My biggest need immediately is:
- My plans for immediately after the divorce are:
- My educational or employment needs are:
- The property/assets I want most are:
- The biggest disadvantage(s) to the assets I want is/are:
- My spouse's most immediate need is:
- The property/assets he/she wants most are:
- The biggest disadvantage(s) to the assets I think he/she wants is/are:

Determine Your Negotiating Potential

Now evaluate the amount of crossover you see between what you perceive as your spouse's immediate needs and favored assets against your own. Is there any potential for conflict? If there is, you can bet that it will be difficult to meet your needs and stay on friendly terms with your spouse—at least during the immediate pre- and post-dissolution period.

Make sure you have considered the expenses attached to an asset, such as future taxes on profits, sales charges, and deferred and ongoing maintenance costs for real estate. If you need to rely on assets to live on, attempt to get a larger share of any income-producing liquid assets before you accept non-liquid income producers such as real estate holdings. Those types of assets often come with on-going expenses to maintain them. Financial assets do not.

Build A Team

Don't be afraid to use counseling professionals, clergy, or support groups. Divorce is one of the most stressful events that a person can go through. Utilize the support from your friends and family. If you have children, they may also need extra support and consideration to help them cope with the radical changes in their world.

Avoid emotional decision making. Your ex-spouse is probably one of the best experts in the world in knowing which of your buttons to push to get you to react. Consider carefully the long term financial impact of each settlement offer proposed to you.

Talk each settlement proposal over with your attorney. He or she is your principal advocate and ally in this process. Here also a financial planner can provide valuable feedback, particularly in long term marriages or where there is a lot of money at stake. Discuss complex tax issues with an accountant. Good communication with all your team members is the key to understanding what constitutes a fair settlement.

CHAPTER SIXTEEN
Can You Avoid Going To Trial

Perhaps. If you are up against the trial schedule, it is time to think through the following questions:

1. Is his/her best offer within $5,000-$10,000 of the bottom line settlement I am seeking? If so, think about one final settlement negotiation with your spouse. Remind him or her of the legal costs on his or her side also. Most cases which are tried end up costing a minimum of $10,000 in attorney fees and other experts for the trial alone. Complex and lengthy cases can cost much, much more.

2. What specific items of your asset base are important to your spouse but have not seemingly been available to him/her? Can you see yourself trading those items for something else? In other words, are there any carrots left in your bag?

3. Is there anything about his/her stance that is unjust or capricious? Is it possible the probability of trial may have mellowed your spouse enough so that he or she is more reasonable?

4. Have you made a conscious effort to agree on as many items as possible? The more items you can agree upon, the easier it will be for your attorney to get your case resolved with or without a trial. Don't get hung up on small items such as who gets the lawn-mower or freezer. Focus your attention on items without which your lifestyle would be drastically altered.

5. Does your attorney think the other side's last ditch offer is fair? Ask your attorney what he or she thinks the range of outcomes might be if you don't accept the offer and the case goes to trial. Also ask your attorney what he or she thinks are the strengths and weaknesses of the other side's offer.

6. Is there anything else you can do to settle out of court?

Should You Keep The Reins?

Remember, once in trial, control has been taken away from you. The outcome will depend in part upon how persuasively your attorney presents the case and how realistic your position is. When the facts are before the judge, an opinion will be rendered. And at that point you will just have to live with the result, whatever it may be.

CHAPTER SEVENTEEN
Odds And Important Ends

No doubt you still have a few questions left about the divorce process. This chapter will attempt to answer those we hear most often:

How will I file my income tax returns during the divorce period?

If you are single by year end, you will be able to file as a single taxpayer and avoid a possible "marriage tax penalty" incurred by the Married Filing Jointly tax system. And, more importantly, you can avoid assuming any tax liability as a result of actions taken by your spouse. If you are not single by year end, consider filing as Married Filing Separately. This will safeguard you from liability for your spouse's tax bill and, if you are the lower earner spouse, may be more beneficial to you than filing a joint return.

If you have been separated for more than six months, live in the family residence, provide more than half the support for a qualified dependent who lives with you and have paid more than one half of the household costs, you can file as Head of Household. This is a lower tax rate schedule than Married Filing Separately. Married Filing Jointly offers the lowest tax rate schedule and should be considered if you are certain your spouse has been honest with regard to income and deductions. If you don't think he or she has been 100% up-front with income and expense activities as reported on your joint 1040, ask your attorney to draw up an indemnification agreement for your spouse to sign if he or she wants your cooperation in filing a joint return.

Calculate your taxes both filing jointly and separately to see which would save you the most money.

Do I have to keep my married name?

Relax, you don't have to keep it if you don't want it. You can change your name back to your maiden name or that of a previous spouse or use whatever name you wish as long as you do not intend to defraud. Your attorney should be able to answer any questions you have in this area.

Some women want to keep their ex-spouse's name due to

having children with that name. Some decide not to ever change their name again even if they remarry in the future. Your spouse cannot prevent you from keeping his name. It is very common these days to meet married couples with different surnames.

Do I need to have an attorney to get a divorce?

The answer here is no, but.... If the property is simple, there are no children, no pensions, no debts, no need for a disparate division of assets and/or spousal support, and you and your spouse agree on everything, perhaps you can do it yourself. However, we just would not recommend it. Chances are somewhere down the road, you are going to remember something overlooked that an astute attorney would have caught.

Can my spouse and I share an attorney?

You can, but how can that person be an advocate for you? It is impossible to do the best for each of you if there are any disputes involved. The attorney's only choice in such situations is to recommend a middle ground compromise which may not be warranted. There is a true conflict of interest in representing two opposing parties, and ethically an attorney cannot do that. You deserve an attorney whose concern is you and you alone.

Who determines how much child support will be paid?

Each state has its own guidelines. The state of Washington has a child support schedule which takes into consideration each parent's income and applies a percent formula against each. This formula assures that one parent won't be unfairly burdened while the other parent escapes responsibility. Again, check with your attorney regarding the law in your state.

FINANCIAL PLANNING *from* WE *to* ME

How do I collect child support from the non-custodial parent if he or she quits paying?

Child support collection laws are in place in every state. In the state of Washington, there are three legal methods available to collect back child support. You can hire a private attorney to ask a judge to order the errant parent to make his or her payment. Those who do not pay voluntarily have their paychecks garnished, thus taking the choice about paying away from them. Your second option is your state's Office of Support Enforcement which offers collection assistance and is free of charge in Washington State. OSE (also now known as DCS—the Division of Child Support) is a collection agency that uses all of the methods available to private attorneys as well as its own resources and can be located under the Department of Social & Health Services in the telephone directory listing of state offices. The third method for child support collection is to use the services of the prosecuting attorney which are usually not available except for welfare parents.

What if my spouse leaves and takes all the money?

Your attorney can petition the court to order your spouse to pay temporary support—both spousal and child. This is one important reason to gather together as soon as possible all the information you can regarding the expenses necessary to maintain the house as well as allowing the children (if any) to continue in their normal routines. You can also have your attorney petition for the transfer or release of a lump sum of cash for expenses.

What can I do to reduce legal costs?

Be informed. Review the resource list at the back of this book. Read as many of the books listed as you can find. Visit the local law library and ask if your state has a family law handbook. Organize your expenses, assets, and debts before you first meet with an attorney. Create a flow chart which lists date of marriage, addresses and length of residence in all the places you've lived, education during the marriage, and jobs held along with hours worked, salary, and term of employment. Do the same for your spouse.

Never withhold information from your attorney which may be material to the case. Your integrity must be unassailable. If the case proceeds to trial, partial truths will surface, and you and your attorney will be placed at a disadvantage if you have not provided the necessary information.

Are my legal fees tax deductible?

Some are—some aren't. This is one reason to bring a financial advisor onto your team. You can deduct legal, financial, or accounting fees relating to tax issues, determination of alimony (for payee only), or determination of the estate impact of certain property settlements. Fees to appraisers and actuaries also are deductible if their work results in determining the correct amount of tax or estate value of a pension benefit. Court costs and normal legal fees are not deductible. This includes determination of child support and custody, compilation of financial data and property recommendations. The cost of specific advice relating to retention of income-producing property can be added to the basis of such property. Keep in mind that the total tax deductible expenses still have to exceed 2% of your adjustable gross income in order to actually give you a tax benefit. One strategy that can be used to maximize the tax benefit from fees that are deductible is to have those fees paid for by the lower income spouse, while awarding that spouse a higher level of maintenance in that year to effectively cover the fees. In some instances this can result in an effective "double deduction" for both spouses. The effectiveness depends on the relative incomes of the spouses and the amount of the payee spouse's Schedule A deductions.

What if my spouse doesn't give me the total due for both child support and alimony?

The law states that any dollars paid will first be used to satisfy child support and any remaining incomplete payment will be construed as alimony. This law protects the receiver of the payment by allocating the dollars first to the tax free child support obligation and last to fully taxable alimony.

Will I have to pay taxes on any assets or property transferred to me as a result of the property division?

Most property is transferred without any tax gain or loss recognition if the property is transferred within one year of the marriage or is related to the termination of the marriage. To qualify for the second rule, the transfer must be required by the separation or divorce agreement and be accomplished within six years after the date of divorce. You can owe income taxes on IRAs if you withdraw funds rather than have them transferred between spouses or if you take direct receipt of pension dollars transferred by QDRO. This can be avoided by having the pension proceeds transferred directly to an IRA custodian or having your spouse's IRA registered in your name by the custodian. Watch out for holdings of real property in Canada or other foreign nations, as the tax laws are different. Discuss this with your attorney and a tax professional.

The transfer of Series EE bonds, however, is an exception. The spouse transferring bonds in his/her name to the other spouse must include on his/her tax return, in the year of the

Chapter Seventeen—Odds And Important Ends

divorce, all untaxed accrued interest. The new owner of the bonds will therefore have a new basis in the bonds and will only have to pay taxes on interest accrued after the date of the divorce and then only when the bonds are cashed in. This is a good reason to try to leave EE bonds with the original owner spouse if possible.

Do I have to pay taxes on my spousal maintenance?

Unfortunately yes. You are responsible to the IRS for the payment of income taxes on any spousal support that you received. Contact your local IRS office and request instructions and forms for filing quarterly tax estimates. These payments are due April 15, June 15, September 15, and January 15, and failure to make adequate estimated payments can result in tax penalties.

Are gifts considered joint property?

Sometimes. Consider, for example, the purchase of diamond earrings during the marriage. Were they meant to be an investment or were they an anniversary gift from your husband? This may be an item on the negotiation table or deferred to the decision of the judge.

Should I see a therapist?

It is up to you. Many people going through a divorce seek professional help in working through this emotionally difficult period. A good therapist can be invaluable in helping you get past the emotional issues so that you can make better decisions, aid in the healing process, and help you to understand what went wrong with the relationship so that you try to avoid similar pitfalls in the future.

Should I go through a mediation process?

If you're having trouble communicating with your spouse, divorce mediation may help. This can be effective if both spouses are willing to negotiate in good faith. However, if the dollar amount at stake is large enough, court may be the only way to get a fair settlement from a stubborn spouse. Mediation may not be appropriate if your spouse is controlling and/or abusive. Litigation costs, especially in a major city, can easily run $10,000-$20,000 or more for each side. You alone must evaluate the financial impact of compromising on a settlement rather than duking it out in front of a judge. Good financial and legal advice can help you make this tough decision.

Why can't my attorney give me financial advice?

Attorneys have not been trained to be financial whizzes. A few have, but they are rare. Even if your attorney can compute your pension values, calculate taxes owed on assets, advise you on reasonable expense levels, validate the nature of various assets, and project your future financial situation, he or she cannot testify on your behalf as to those facts. As an advocate for you, your attorney is not an objective third party and therefore cannot offer expert witness testimony to help your spouse, the opposing attorney or a judge come to an equitable conclusion.

CHAPTER EIGHTEEN
Choosing Your Attorney

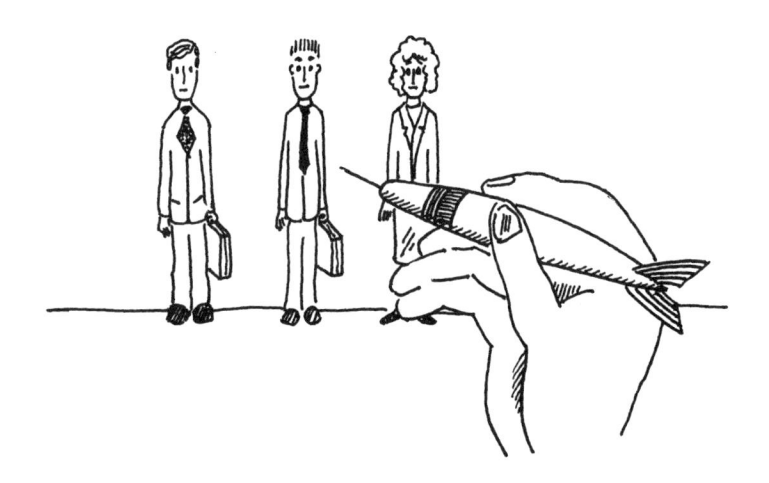

This is a difficult but important first step. Most people start out by asking friends who have had direct experience with divorce or who know people who have gone through the divorce process. This is a start, but keep in mind that the answers you get might be vividly colored by the individual's emotional response to the whole process. Remember, everyone's situation is different.

Ask Other Professionals

A better way would be to call several associated professionals—accountants who value businesses, financial planners who work with divorcing couples, or your family attorney. You want to get the best advocate you can during this stressful time.

Optimally, you will find an attorney who is brilliant in the courtroom, a skilled negotiator, tough enough to stand up for what is in your best interests, financially astute, and concerned about your emotional health. This won't be easy, but then again, you can help provide the last two elements by hiring a financial expert and seeing a therapist.

The Third Degree

Asking the following questions will help you make a choice you won't regret later.

1. What are your fees both in the office and in the courtroom? How do you charge for your time? At what rate do you bill out your staff's time? What is the range of fees for cases like mine which are settled pre-trial? What is the average length of a trial and what would your fees be for two days in court? Do you anticipate other expert witness fees?

2. Will you handle the case and if I am not talking to you, to whom would I be talking? Most attorneys have able assistants who gather much of the data, organize the case, and perform the routine type of filings.

3. How large a retainer do you require? How will I know when it has been exhausted? What about other experts? How will they be paid? What is your billing practice?

4. If this is a Washington State case, ask the attorney if he or she is familiar with the 1989 Gender and Justice Report which discusses gender prejudice in the courtroom. Ask what in his or her opinion would be a fair settlement for a long term marriage where one of the spouses is under-employed or

unemployed and the other a high wage earner. You will probably get a couple of different answers depending on the assumption of the size of the asset base for the hypothetical situation. While this may not be your situation, it will give you a clear idea of the attorney's position on the issue of "equitable" settlements.

5. If yours is a marriage as described above, ask if the attorney has ever utilized a financial advisor to prepare a disparity report showing each spouse's potential to further accumulate or dissipate his or her asset base.

6. Ask what you can do to keep your legal costs within reason. How much of the legwork can you do yourself?

Remember, It's Your Future

The outcome of your divorce will be influenced by several critical areas: the facts at hand, your financial needs, case law, the skills of your attorney as a negotiator and litigator and, if the case goes to trial, the astuteness of the judge. Be knowledgeable about the relevant facts, don't withhold information, and be reasonable. Doing your best in these areas will help your attorney do his or her best also.

CHAPTER NINETEEN
Choosing A Financial Advisor

Choosing a financial advisor to help you through your pending divorce is not the same as finding one to help you plan your retirement future. The dissolution financial advisor must be savvy in all the areas previously discussed in this book. More than just talking knowledge is needed. He or she also needs experience in working with attorneys and their clients as well as the "pleasure" of being an expert witness during numerous trials.

Needle In The Haystack

Finding this advisor can be like looking for a needle in a haystack, as most financial advisors do not work in this area. It is challenging work with sometimes emotional clients. It can also be punishing if it ends with the opposing counsel trying to make chopped liver of the financial advisor's testimony during a trial.

Your attorney is the best source—that is, if he or she has faced the reality that it is critical in certain cases to incorporate a financial advisor on the support team. Many of our dissolution clients were referred by their attorneys who had either used us in the past, been opposing counsel on a case, or who had heard of us from other attorneys.

Choose carefully. The integrity your planner brings to the process must be absolute and impeccable. At this point in your life, you may be vulnerable to money abuses. The last thing you need is a financial planner who also has reason and motivation to suggest acquisition of certain financial products upon the conclusion of your divorce. Your best protection is to insist on seeing a copy of his/her SEC disclosure brochure. If he or she is involved at all with investments, this brochure should be available. Read it carefully to ensure that the person is not both planner and salesperson for insurance and investment products. Seek a financial advocate who has no temptations which could possibly color any financial recommendations.

Sleuthing For Value

Here is a list of questions to ask the financial advisor:

1. How many years have you participated in giving input and recommendations to divorcing parties?

Chapter Nineteen—Choosing A Financial Advisor

2. How many years have you worked with attorneys and their dissolution clients? How many times have you been officially retained as part of the dissolution team of advisors?

3. Have you been an expert witness in a dissolution trial? What jurisdictions and how many times? What did your testimony involve?

4. What type of assistance do you provide and what kind of documentation can I expect to substantiate my needs?

5. What is your underlying training? Do you have a degree and, if so, in what field? Do you have a financial certification? Do you have any special training relating to divorce?

6. Who is your ideal client—the kind you feel you can help best?

7. What are your hourly fees? Do you charge a different rate for expert testimony? How do you charge for your time? At what rate do you bill out your staff's time? What has the average fee been in cases settled pre-trial?

8. How long does it usually take to prepare a comprehensive disparity report?

9. How much involvement with me will you have and how much through your staff? As with attorneys, most successful financial advisors have able assistants who gather much of the data, organize the case, and structure the routine reports.

10. How large a retainer do you require? How will I know when it has been exhausted? Will other financial experts be required? For which areas? How do you bill?

11. Can you provide me with the names of several individuals with whom you have worked whose situations were similar to mine?

If you are choosing this advisor to help you place or evaluate investments, the following questions are mandatory.

12. Can you provide me with your ADV, Part 2 or a substitute brochure acceptable for use in full disclosure according to the Securities and Exchange Commission?

13. What is your investment advisory background? Ask for his or her Vita. Additionally, for fee only advisors ask what year he or she became a Registered Investment Advisor. Alternatively, if he or she is a commission based advisor, what year did he or she pass the test for a Registered Representative license.

14. What is the source of your income—fees, fees and commissions, or commissions only? If commissions are involved, ask what percentage of the advisor's income is derived from commissions.

15. Ask if you can have the names of three client references.

16. Ask how many clients the advisor has in each of the following age groups: 25-40; 40-65; 65-85. This will help you determine whether he or she will be familiar with investment needs common to individuals in your age group.

Take CARE

Interview at least three planners before making a decision on who appears to be the most competent and trustworthy. Remember, this isn't truly evident until you have spent some time with the planner, and unfortunately that is usually after you have become his or her client. So take CARE with this decision and look for an advisor who is *Credentialed, Accountable, Resourceful, and Experienced* enough to be entrusted with helping you make appropriate financial decisions.

CHAPTER TWENTY
Choosing A Therapist

Choosing a therapist has both similarities to and differences from finding an attorney and financial planner. This person will be helping you through the emotional turmoil of a traumatic life passage.

It is possible that you have been in therapy during difficult times in the marriage and feel that this chapter is superfluous. Read it anyway. The death of a relationship, like the death of a person, often brings about a natural grieving process. However, most people who have been through a divorce agree that dealing with death is easier. You may find you need professional support even more during the actual divorce process.

Getting Help

It can be difficult to find a good fit with a counselor. Use the "word-of-mouth" referral network. Ask people you know if they can give you names of good psychotherapists. Your physician and staff are also a good resource. Check to see if your health insurance plan covers mental health counseling and if so, which providers are covered by your plan.

It is wise to interview potential counselors in person. A good therapist demonstrates respect, genuine interest, warmth and, hopefully, a sense of humor. You are looking for someone who will give you feedback and a sense of safety and confidence. Find someone you like. Trust your "gut" feelings.

Therapeutic Probes

Do not be afraid to ask questions. The following are some suggestions. Make a list before the interview using these as guidelines and adding your own.

1. What is your educational background?

2. Are you licensed at the state level? If his or her degree is a Master's level, ask if the person is a Certified Mental Health Counselor, which requires passing a test given by the state. If his or her degree is a Ph.D., the person needs to have a license as a clinical psychologist. Psychiatrists are medical doctors.

3. How long have you been in practice? What kind of clients do you work with? Do you specialize?

4. What is your approach to psychotherapy? Your beliefs and models? How do you "do" therapy?

5. What do you charge? How is payment made? Do you take third party payments (insurance)? If so, ask for an explanation of the loss of confidentiality inherent in using health insurance.

Chapter 20—Choosing A Therapist

6. How long is each session? How often will we meet? Do you have a sense of how long I might need to be in therapy?

7. What are your beliefs about divorce?

8. If your spirituality is important to you, ask if the therapist is comfortable with your spiritual beliefs.

Confidentiality is the cornerstone of psychotherapy. Therefore the counselor cannot give you names of former clients as references. He or she can, however, give you names of other therapists as references.

CHAPTER TWENTY-ONE
After The Dark, Comes Light

At some point your divorce will be final—the last piece of paper signed, the final court orders filed. You may experience elation, sadness, resignation or a host of other emotions. Hopefully, you will experience a great sense of relief as you close one chapter in your life and open a new one.

Much of the financial uncertainty of the separation period will end with the final divorce settlement. Now you know exactly what property you have to work with and what child support and/or spousal maintenance levels will need to be paid out or be available as income. It may not be what you wanted if you are the payer or what you needed if you are the payee, but it probably is what you are going to have to live with.

Help Yourself

There are steps you can take to help yourself start building a new financial future. If you have been out of the financial loop during your marriage, make an effort to educate yourself about personal financial matters. Take a class at a community college or read a few books on financial planning.

Now that you're on your own, it may be appropriate for you to review the following items as they relate to your specific financial planning needs:

1. **Life Insurance**: Up until now we talked about life insurance on ex-spouses to insure payment of income streams in the event of death of the payer. You may also need to insure yourself if you have dependents that will require more money to support them than available from your asset base.

2. **Health Insurance**: We've discussed this in Chapter Thirteen. Solid insurance coverage should be an integral part of protecting your asset base from medical expenses.

3. **Disability Insurance**: While we did not discuss disability insurance for you, it may be important. If you are single and receiving an income which would disappear if you did not work, it would behoove you to consider carrying disability insurance on yourself.

Chapter Twenty-One—After the Dark, Comes Light

4. **Nursing Home Insurance**: If you are over 50, you may wish to consider this type of insurance also. Long term care expenses can erode assets faster than the eye can see or at least that will be what it seems like when those care providers charge upwards of $3,000 per month. Like any insurance, one must weigh the probabilities of using it versus the cost and risk of not having it. If you have an elderly parent, this may be something you want to discuss with them also.

5. **Other Insurance**: If you have assets of such value that they exceed the liability coverage you have elected in your basic homeowners and automotive policies, you may either need to raise your limits under those policies or you may need to acquire an "umbrella" liability policy. This kind of coverage is relatively inexpensive but necessary to protect you against potential lawsuits. Your auto insurance and homeowners insurance should be reviewed to determine the most cost-effective mix of coverages versus deductibles.

6. **Investment Mix**: How your assets are allocated will have a lot to do with how fast your money will grow. The most important element is to determine if the mix between fixed income assets and growth assets is appropriate given your goals for investment returns.

In the resource section at the back of this volume we have listed an easy to read primer, *Keys to Controlling Your Financial Destiny: Financial Insider Tips Every Woman Needs to Know*, by Kathleen Cotton and Rachel Paysse. This book could be useful to you in helping explain the basics relating to organizing and planning your financial future. Remember, you are the sole financial decision maker now. Make your decisions sound ones.

Create A Spending Plan

Budgeting will be just as important now as it was during the separation period. If you are the support payer, you need to include those costs in your cash flow. With the property division finalized you likely will need to begin to replace household furniture and appliances that ended up on your spouse's side of the table. However, beware of the dreaded credit trap! Overspending in those first intoxicating or gray days of singledom can hurt your cash flow for years to come. Also do not neglect to make annual savings a fixed expense equal to 10-15 percent of your gross income. The ideal place for this activity to take place is within an IRA or employer sponsored retirement plan.

Immediate Post Divorce Issues

In previous chapters we have touched on a number of subjects that need to be addressed in the divorce process. Some you could not act upon until now and others should have been dealt with during the dissolution process. Following are action items to do now:

1. **Automobiles**: You should get the original title to the auto(s) and have it transferred into your individual name. Titles to automobiles must be transferred within 15 days of entry of the Decree of Dissolution (State of Washington), otherwise, the state will charge $100.00 for the title transfer. For autos newer than 1986, you will need a statement showing the odometer reading of the car signed by your former spouse. If you live in an emissions control area (like Seattle) you will also need a passed emissions test report within the last six months. Check with your state's Department of Licensing for their requirements.

2. **Automobile Insurance**. You should notify the insurer that you are now divorced and secure your own individual

Chapter Twenty-One—After the Dark, Comes Light

automobile insurance policy as soon as possible after the entry of the Decree of Dissolution.

3. **Life Insurance.** You should notify your life insurance company of the divorce and request that your former spouse be removed as a beneficiary of the insurance proceeds, if you haven't already done so. If you or your spouse are required to maintain life insurance insuring a child support and/or maintenance obligation, then that particular life insurance company should be notified of the nature and extent of the obligation. The company should also be sent, by registered mail, a copy of the Decree of Dissolution outlining the obligation.

4. **Other Insurance.** All other insurance companies such as homeowner's insurance, personal liability insurance, etc. should be notified of the entry of the Decree of Dissolution so that appropriate adjustments to the insurance can be made. If you are eligible for health coverage through a private or group policy that offers comparable coverage at a lower cost than through COBRA, you may want to make a change here too.

5. **Investments.** Investments, such as limited partnerships, general partnerships, etc., should be notified and sent a copy of the Decree of Dissolution so that the company can make appropriate changes to ensure notification to you and your spouse, issue reporting forms to the federal government for tax purposes, and change registration of ownership.

6. **Wills.** You should have a Trust Will prepared for you if you have minor children. If you are a Washington State resident and do not change your will leaving your former spouse named as beneficiary, the statutes for succession of property under a will do not permit your property to pass to your former spouse. In other words, your property would pass as though you had no

former spouse. This could substantially disrupt your own estate planning, especially in cases where children's financial needs are concerned. Inheritance laws do vary from state to state, so be sure to ask your attorney regarding the statutes in your home state.

7. **Personal Property.** When your spouse takes possession of any personal property under your control, make sure that a receipt listing all of the items taken is signed and dated by your spouse to prevent any future misunderstandings about the property transferred.

8. **Qualified Domestic Relations Order.** If you are awarded pension benefits of any nature or kind, then a Qualified Domestic Relations Order (QDRO) must be entered and a copy sent to the plan administrator. The Plan Administrator will notify you by letter of receipt of the QDRO and a proposed time table for notifying you that the QDRO is technically correct. If you have not received a letter from the Plan Administrator regarding the procedure for qualification or a notice indicating that the QDRO is qualified within three months of entry of the Decree of Dissolution, then there is a problem in your case which needs to be addressed immediately.

You do not want to be in a situation where the QDRO is not entered; otherwise you may have no pension/retirement benefits. The only pension benefits you will receive from your spouse's pension or 401(k) plan, etc., are pursuant to the provisions in the Qualified Domestic Relations Order. As the non-employee spouse, you may be entitled to take that benefit early under a subsidized retirement program. If you begin your benefit early, that benefit may be increased when the employee, your former spouse, retires. If you start the benefit before he or she retires, however, it may be increased at a later date only if

Chapter Twenty-One—After the Dark, Comes Light

your ex-spouse retires before normal retirement age. If your former spouse does not retire before normal retirement, then your benefit may not be increased. Check with the pension administrator of the plan in question.

If you haven't yet completed the changes discussed in the preceding paragraphs, don't delay further. This is the time to update your will and estate planning, change your life insurance and retirement account beneficiaries and/or obtain life insurance coverage on the support payer to protect against loss of child support or spousal maintenance in case of his or her premature demise. Don't let this wait too long, as it will be easier to work with your ex-spouse in establishing your ownership of a life insurance policy on him or her while the need for such coverage is still fresh in your ex's mind. Every day you wait exposes you to additional risk that your ex-spouse may become uninsurable due to health reasons.

You May Need A Financial Professional

If you have not yet consulted a qualified financial professional regarding your situation, you may wish to do so now, particularly if you are receiving a large lump sum of cash from the sale of property or a retirement plan distribution. You may need to set aside dedicated dollars for future taxes, invest the proceeds for your future, or tap those assets for immediate income. In any event, a financial advisor may be able to help you sort it out.

If your situation mirrors any of the following, you should see a financial advisor immediately.

1. You are going to receive a QDRO distribution of dollars from your ex-spouse's qualified retirement accounts.

2. You are trying to decide how much, if any, of your QDRO distribution to take receipt of without a 10% penalty and how much to have transferred to an IRA of your choice.

Ideally, you can meet with the advisor prior to your attorney completing the QDRO paperwork and submitting it to the retirement plan in question. This is critical.

3. You will receive ownership of your ex-spouse's IRA account(s) as a result of the dissolution.

4. You are under 59-1/2 and need to start a SEPP (Systematic Early Periodic Payments) from your IRA(s) in such a manner as to avoid the pre 59-1/2 10% penalty.

5. You will be a recipient of house sale proceeds and will need to determine what to do with them until you either purchase a replacement residence or decide to invest the funds in other ways.

6. You will be awarded stocks or bonds your ex-spouse has always looked after.

7. You need assistance in determining how much of your property and income settlement to set aside for current needs such as retraining or anticipated monthly expenses.

8. You want to establish a relationship with an advisor to help you over the rough spots as you start out on a new financial excursion or if you have little or no investment knowledge and are a sitting duck target for investment salespersons.

Run, don't walk, to a qualified financial advisor. Go back if necessary to Chapter 19 for tips on how to select that advisor.

Chapter Twenty-One—After the Dark, Comes Light

Moving Forward

We recently found the following quote and think it describes aptly what needs to happen now:

"I find the great thing in this world is not so much where we stand as in what direction we are moving. To reach the port of heaven, we must sail, sometimes with the wind and sometimes against it—but we must sail, and not drift, nor lie at anchor."

Oliver Wendell Holmes is the author of that great piece of wisdom.

The information in this chapter is brief and certainly does not give you in-depth exposure to the types of educational issues you may require to become a financially savvy and independent person, but it is easy to tidy up your financial act. Are you wondering how we can make such a bold statement? No, we don't know you yet, but we believe in you. We believe in the value of financial organization, knowledge, and a plan. That's what we want to bring to you.

You are just beginning, again. You, like many others, have come a long way during your life experiences. You've been tested and survived one of life's most trying curve balls—divorce. At this juncture another door is opening for you, a door where there will be many choices you must make. Remember, you are now the master of your situation, and the choices you make will determine how well you face new opportunities. As the door to the future opens further and the light begins to grow brighter and brighter, so does the need to accept responsibility; specifically, to accept responsibility for being financially literate.

We have had a great time in putting together this book for you. We hope it has helped get you through your divorce with your sanity intact. This book can help you avoid making financial mistakes you would regret. One of the easiest financial mistakes to make is the mistake of procrastination. To provide you with some motivation to move forward, we'd like to share the following story:

"Once upon a time, there were two horsewomen and one horseman riding across an arid plain. They were very tired and eager to make their camp for the night. As they rode a voice spoke to them, "Halt and dismount your horses." Never having heard a voice before in the desert, no one believed what each had heard so they continued on. Again, they heard the voice speak with the same message, and they looked at each other and knew it was real. Frightened, they obeyed the command and stopped dead in their tracks. As they got off their horses, they heard the voice for the third time saying, "Reach down and pick up some pebbles and put them in your pockets." They did not understand this message but they did as instructed and stuck a handful of rocks in their pockets.

Not hearing anything more, the group mounted their horses and commenced riding to their camp. Once again the voice spoke, "Tomorrow morning you will be both happy and sad as a result of obeying my command." As you can guess, they did not understand any of this sequence of events and because it was late, they hurried on to make camp for the night.

In the morning, as they pulled on their pants, they put their hands in their pockets and touched the pebbles which now felt round, smooth and shiny. When the man and women pulled out the contents, they saw diamonds and rubies and pearls. Then they remembered what the voice in the desert had said, "Tomorrow morning you will be both happy and sad." They were happy that they had picked up as many pebbles as they had and sad they had not picked up more."

Chapter Twenty-One—After the Dark, Comes Light

Yes, there is a moral to this story, and it is a simple one. We hope that regardless of whether you are male or female, young or old, five years from now you will be able to say, "I'm glad I did all that I could during my divorce and immediately thereafter to meet my financial needs and get my new future off to a good start." We don't want you to say, "I wish I had taken action sooner."

Good luck. We hope you have profited by our shared words of wisdom and will continue to profit as you move forward into your new life.

RESOURCE DIRECTORY

Books

While there are many books written on the subject of divorce and money, the books I have listed are from my personal collection.

A Women's Guide to Divorce and Decision Making, Robertson, Christina. Fireside, 1980.

The Dollars and Sense of Divorce: The Financial Guide for Women, Briles, Judith. MasterMedia 1988.

Divorce & Money: Everything You Need to Know About Dividing Property, Woodhouse, Violet and Felton-Collins, Victoria with Blakeman, M.C. Nolo Press 1992.

Financial Fitness Through Divorce: A Guide to the Financial Realities of Divorce, Lewin, Elizabeth S, CFP. Facts on File, 1987.

Mediate Your Divorce: A Guide to Cooperative Custody, Property and Support Agreements, Blades, Joan. Prentice Hall, 1985.

Practical Divorce Solutions, Sherman, Charles Ed. Nolo Press, 1988.

The Survivor Manual for Women in Divorce: 150 Questions and Answers About Your Rights, Wilson, Carol Ann and Schilling, Edwin III, Esq. Quantum Press, 1990.

The Financial Guide to Divorce: Everything you Need to Know for Financial Strategies During (And After) Divorce, Johansen, Frances, CFP. United Resource Press, 1990.

Keys to Controlling Your Financial Destiny: Financial Insider Tips Every Woman Needs to Know, Cotton, Kathleen, CFP and Paysse, Rachel, CFP, Wealth Books, 1990.

Spend Your Way to Wealth, Cotton, Kathleen, CFP, Wealth Books, 1992.

General Resources

University or County law libraries

Family Law Reporter, Bureau of National Affairs

American Academy of Matrimonial Lawyers, 312-263-6477

Domestic Violence Hot Line 1-800-333-7233

American Association for Marriage and Family Therapy, 202-452-0109

National Child Support Enforcement Association, 202-624-8180

U.S. Department of Health and Human Services, Office of Support Enforcement, 610 Executive Blvd. Rockville, MD 20852

American Society of Appraisers (business), 303-758-6158

FINANCIAL PLANNING *from* WE *to* ME

Appraisal Institute (real estate), 312-335-4100

Bankcard Holders of America (information service), 703-481-1110

Internal Revenue Service (tax information and forms), 800-829-1040

Institute of Certified Financial Planners (advisors who are licensed to hold the CFP designation), 800-282-7526

National Association of Personal Financial Advisors (fee-only advisors with credentials, education and experience), 800-366-2732

National Foundation for Consumer Credit (referral to local Consumer Credit Offices), 800-388-2227

Social Security Administration (work benefits and history), 800-234-5772

Military Information Resources

Army: Defense Financial and Accounting Service, Attn: FINCL-G, Indianapolis, IN 46249

Navy: Defense Financial and Accounting Service, Code DG, Celebreeze Federal Building, Cleveland, OH 44199-2055

Air Force: Defense Finance and Accounting Service, Attn: JA, Denver, CO 80279

Marine Corps: Defense Finance and Accounting Service, Code DG, Kansas City, MO 64197-0001

Coast Guard: General Law Division, G-LGL, United States Coast Guard, 2100 Second Street S.W., Washington, D.C. 20593

Washington State Specific Resources

Divorce Guide for Washington State, Patterson, Mark T. Self Counsel Press, 1989.

Divorce in Washington, Halverson, Lowell K. and Kydd, John W. Eagle House Press, 1992.

Family Law in Washington State, Northwest Women's Law Center, 1991. $6.00. Invaluable resource with resource citations for cities and counties throughout Washington State. Order from 119 South Main Street, Suite 330, Seattle WA 98104 or call 206-621-7691.

Northwest Women's Law Center for attorney and community resource referrals. 206-621-7691.

Domestic Violence Hotline 1-800-562-6025

Washington Coalition of Sexual Assault Programs 206-753-4634

Divorce Lifeline, 6920 220th St. S.W., Mountlake Terrace WA 98043 (206) 624-2959. This is a program of Lutheran Social Services of Washington. Call for location nearest you.

GLOSSARY

While not all of the following terms have been referenced in this book, the terms and the definitions are common financial jargon and you will encounter them as you read and learn more about financial issues.

Adjustable Rate Mortgage (ARM): A form of real estate loan in which the interest and monthly payment are periodically adjusted up or down based on current interest rates, rather than remaining fixed. Popular during periods of low or declining interest rates, they lose their appeal when interest rates, and monthly payments, head skywards.

Balance Sheet: In a business, this is simply a written accounting of the company's net worth, i.e. all the company's assets and liabilities.

Balloon Payment: A large extra or final payment due on a mortgage or lease. An expensive surprise for the forgetful.

Banked Vacation or Sick Pay: Some employers allow their employees to "bank" a portion of their unused sick and vacation pay into investment type accounts. Usually there are strict restrictions on how and when the employee can access these funds.

Capital Gains Tax: Income generated from the sale of assets is considered capital gains. As of March 1995 the maximum tax rate on capital gains is 28%, which offers tax savings to high income tax payers. A favorite target for tax reformers in Congress, this tax law is likely to change, so always consult your tax advisor for current regulations.

Child Support: The financial support due from a parent to his or her child(ren). This is calculated for both parents based on their comparative income levels and paid by the non-custodian parent to the custodial parent. Depending on your point of view, these dollars are (A) bleeding you dry or (B) just not enough.

Closing Costs: The costs incurred when a piece of real estate is transferred from one entity to another. They can be borne by the buyer, the seller, or both.

COBRA: a.k.a. the Congressional Omnibus Budget Reconciliation Act. This law requires employers to provide ex-employees or the soon-to-be ex-spouses of employees with an option to continue their group medical coverage for 18 or 36 months respectively. The cost of the plan is paid by the individual, not the employer.

Collateral: An asset pledged against a loan. If a default occurs, the collateral may be forfeited to the lender. For this reason, the collateral and the loan should be treated as a package deal in the property division.

Community Property: In a community property state such as Washington, all goods and/or income acquired during the marriage by either spouse. This includes secret Las Vegas bank accounts with your big slot machine winnings. Inheritances and gifts are considered separate property unless commingled with the community dollars—so hang on tight to that inheritance from Uncle Joe.

Cost Basis: This is what it cost you to buy an asset. It includes improvements in the case of a real asset. The taxable gain (what the IRS gets to tax) is the difference between the value of the asset and the cost basis. If you ever end up selling the asset, you'll owe the taxes, so pay attention to what the cost basis is.

Defined Benefit Plan: A type of tax-qualified retirement plan that promises a specific monthly benefit that is calculated by a formula usually based on years of service and average income. The employee may pay part of the cost through payroll deductions, or the employer may foot the entire bill.

Defined Contribution Plan: A type of tax-qualified retirement plan where the employer's plan contribution is specifically set (usually by some formula), and the final benefit to the employee varies depending on investment performance. The employee often has the option to receive his or her benefits as an annuity or a lump sum payment. The employee may pay part of the cost through payroll deductions, or the employer may foot the entire bill. This type of plan includes money purchase plans, target benefit plans, and profit sharing plans.

Deferred Compensation Plan: A plan that allows an employee to elect to defer receipt of part of his or her current compensation until a specific date or action in the future. The employee is not taxed on the compensation until it is received. Typically these plans are not formally funded; rather the employee is in effect a creditor of the company. These are often used as sweeteners for highly paid executives to give them greater opportunity for tax deferral than regular pension plans allow.

Depreciation: The gradual decline in the value of real asset over time. The IRS lets you deduct a portion of the depreciation of business property or investment real estate as an expense, even though it is not "out-of-pocket." Depreciation

Glossary

should be added back in to determine the real income generated by a business or rental property. Beware! Depreciation taken also reduces the cost basis (q.v.) in the property and will be subject to recapture (q.v.) when the property is sold.

Employee Stock Option Plan (ESOP): A plan which allows the employee to acquire shares of the company's stock on a tax qualified basis. Often used in conjunction with other types of retirement plans.

401(k) Plan: A tax-qualified retirement plan that is funded principally through elective contributions made by the employees on a pre-tax basis. Employers may also offer some form of a matching contribution up to a set amount or percentage. The employee is not taxed on either contributions or plan earnings until they are withdrawn. Offers certain special tax advantaged withdrawal methods not available to IRA accounts. May include features for loans or hardship withdrawals. There is a maximum limit to the amount of pre-tax dollars an employee can contribute to 401(k) plans each year—consult your tax advisor.

403(b) Plan (TSAs): A tax-qualified retirement plan available to employees of schools, hospitals, and non-profit organizations that is funded through elective contributions by the employees on a pre-tax basis. The employee is not taxed on contributions or plan earnings until they are withdrawn. Can be invested in annuities or mutual funds. Offers certain special catch-up provisions to allow older employees to maximize their lifetime contributions. There is a maximum limit to the amount of pre-tax dollars an employee can contribute to 403(b) plans each year—consult your tax advisor.

Individual Retirement Account (IRA): A tax-advantaged account that allows persons who qualify to make tax deductible contributions of up to $2,000 each year. Other persons can make non-deductible contributions of up to the same amount. Everyone enjoys the benefit of tax deferred earnings on the account until the funds are withdrawn. A wide variety of investments can be included in an IRA. Consult your tax advisor to see if you qualify for deductible contributions.

Inflation: A general rise in the prices of goods and services over time. A pernicious and constant companion in all of our economic decision making and planning.

Keogh Account: A form of tax-qualified retirement plan designed for sole proprietors and partnerships that allows much larger annual contributions than an IRA. Must include any employees of the business as well as the owner(s).

Limited Partnership: A type of investment in which an individual, along with a lot of other individuals, invests in a business venture through the purchase of units with a set dollar value. The investor has limited liability for the actions of the partnership and receives return through the pass-through of tax deductions, income, and capital gains. The flip side is that losses are also passed through to the investor. Typical partnership investments are real estate, equipment leasing, cable TV systems, etc. Most limited partnerships have not performed up to their original hyped sales pitch and are now worth only a fraction of their original value. They are difficult to sell, with only a limited secondary market.

Liquid Asset: Something that can be quickly and easily turned into cash with little or no chance of loss. Examples—checking and savings accounts, money market accounts, etc. It is important to have three to six months worth of living expenses in liquid assets as an emergency reserve.

Mediation: An increasingly popular method for settling marital conflicts out of court. It brings in a qualified neutral third party to help the disputing couple come to a mutually agreeable settlement.

Personal Exemption: The amount you get to deduct from your taxable income for yourself and each of your dependents. Exemptions for children can be taken by either parent, or if more than one child can be split between the parents. A valuable tax benefit that should be addressed in a settlement.

Points: A percentage of the amount borrowed which is charged as a fee by the lender. Each point is one percent of the loan amount.

Present Value: A financial calculation that converts a current or future stream of payments into an equivalent current lump sum value. This is useful when including a future pension benefit in a property division and should be performed by a qualified professional.

Principal: The actual dollars borrowed in a loan, as opposed to the interest charged on the loan. A loan payment consists of both interest and principal. In the early years of the loan it is mostly interest.

Profit-Sharing Plan: A tax-qualified retirement plan in which the employer bases its contributions to the plan on the profitability of the company. Contributions can and do vary from year to year and can even be zero in some years. This can be a stand-alone plan or an add-on to a 401(k) or money purchase plan.

Qualified Domestic Relations Order (QDRO): A court order used to obtain a portion of a qualified retirement plan in the possession of one spouse and to have the proceeds transferred either to an IRA or other qualified plan for the spouse's benefit or directly to the spouse.

Glossary

Recapture: A means by which the IRS always gets its taxes. The inclusion of previously taken depreciation deductions as ordinary (fully taxable) income when the depreciated property is sold. Also applies to front-loaded spousal support payments.

Spousal Support: Also called maintenance or alimony, this is a transfer payment from the higher income spouse to the lower income spouse. It is deductible to the payer and taxable to the payee.

Stock Options: The right to purchase a set number of shares of a stock at a future date for a set price. The value of the option depends on the difference between the market price for the stock and the exercise price of the option. These are common components in the benefits packages of important employees and can be very valuable.

DID YOU BORROW THIS BOOK?
You deserve your own personal copy!

ORDER FORM
Please send me the following:

		No. of Copies	Total
FINANCIAL PLANNING FROM WE TO ME	@ $9.95 x____		=$_____
Washington residents add state sales tax	@ .81 x____		=$_____
KEYS TO CONTROLLING YOUR FINANCIAL DESTINY: Financial Insider Tips Every Women Needs to Know	@ $4.95 x____		=$_____
Washington residents add state sales tax	@ .40 x____		=$_____

Shipping and Handling Book Rate:
$2.50 first item, $1.50 each additional item   =$_____

S/H on orders in excess of 5 books:
$5.00 flat fee plus actual postage
bill sent with order

TOTAL DUE AND ENCLOSED $

NAME:_____

ADDRESS:_____

CITY/STATE/ZIP:_____

SEND ORDER TO:
Wealth Books
4208 198th Street S.W., Suite 202
Lynnwood, WA 98036
(206) 672-6050